Running from Coyote

Running from Coyote

A White Family among the Navajo

A MEMOIR

Danalee Buhler

iUniverse, Inc.

New York Lincoln Shanghai

Running from Coyote
A White Family among the Navajo

iUniverse books may be ordered through booksellers or by contacting:

iUniverse
2021 Pine Lake Road, Suite 100
Lincoln, NE 68512
www.iuniverse.com
1-800-Authors (1-800-288-4677)

Because of the dynamic nature of the Internet, any Web addresses or links contained in this book may have changed since publication and may no longer be valid.

The views expressed in this work are solely those of the author and do not necessarily reflect the views of the publisher, and the publisher hereby disclaims any responsibility for them.

Cover photo:Danalee and her brother Danny, 1963.

ISBN: 978-0-595-40543-5 (pbk)
ISBN: 978-0-595-84907-9 (ebk)

Printed in the United States of America

For Michael Dean Mitchell

Contents

Part V   *Navajo Taboo: Do not lie about yourself or bad things will come true.*

Acknowledgments

I would like to thank my manuscript readers, especially Lorraine Buhler, for their comments and suggestions. I greatly appreciate Loraine Schacher's editorial review.

I want to thank Joe, Dori and Max for their continued encouragement and support.

Introduction

When I was a little girl, all I wanted to be was Navajo—I desperately wanted to wear a purple velveteen skirt, a shiny silver concho belt, a red velvet blouse, knee-high moccasins, and turquoise jewelry around my neck and wrists. For a seven-year-old, dressing like a Navajo equaled being a Navajo.

From the summer of 1958 until the summer of 1962, my family and I lived on the Navajo Indian reservation in the Four Corners area of New Mexico. We lived in the compound with the other white schoolteachers—behind a six-foot-high chain-link fence. Our compound was composed of the public elementary school, an old abandoned schoolhouse, a couple of single-wide mobile homes, and about a dozen cinder block homes for the schoolteachers.

Shiprock, the reservation town where my family moved in 1958, felt like another world when I first arrived. I soon realized, however, that the schoolteachers' compound was a miniature version of the white world I'd left behind in Texas. Much like my parents, some of the schoolteachers working on the reservation were there because it was more palatable than the white world. The prejudices of white society in the late 1950s made it easier and safer to seek employment on the reservation for those people who lived a nontraditional lifestyle, who were in a racially mixed marriage, or who were older citizens.

Some modern-day Navajo historians label the years in which I lived on the reservation as "the coming-out years." This refers to a time in Navajo history when the Navajo Nation attempted to become more like their white neighbors—more economically stable. Wealth from recently discovered mineral deposits allowed the Navajo Nation to build new schools, larger hospitals, more asphalt roads, and wood-framed houses rather than the traditional hogans. In 1959, the daily newspaper the *Navajo Times* was first published. Printed in English, the newspaper encouraged English as the preferred language.

In 1958 a variety of schools could be found on Indian reservations—church schools, public schools, boarding schools. Shiprock offered all these—it had the Catholic mission school, the public elementary and junior high schools, and Shiprock Indian Boarding School. The boarding school opened in 1903 and remained operational until the 1980s. During the years in which I lived on the reservation, the one thousand Navajo children who attended the massive

Shiprock Indian Boarding School, as well as those who attended the local public schools, were not allowed to speak Navajo, only English.

I use five Navajo taboos to introduce the different parts of this book. There are hundreds of Navajo taboos, and these five are not taken from any one source. To help put the cultural development of the white and Navajo worlds in perspective, each separate part of this book begins with two sentences—one that reflects the white world and one that reflects the Navajo world but both within the same time period.

I began writing my story years ago as a journal, as a way of sharing my unusual childhood with my two children; over the years the journal grew into a book. I have changed the names of the people from Shiprock in this book to protect their privacy.

Much of my story revolves around my grandfather, Skeet, my mother's father, who came to live with us in 1959 and died in 1965. His presence in our home and his hatred of the Navajo helped shape my and my siblings' personalities.

As most parents do at some point in the lives of their children, sharing information about my childhood became the path to discuss bigotry, intolerance, and discrimination. As the story of my childhood unfolded, I realized that I had more to stay about those subjects than I had initially realized.

Growing up in a family with children of mixed ethnic backgrounds was not easy in 1959; it's probably not easy today. The old saying, "That which doesn't kill you makes you stronger," proved true for my siblings and me. When my family left the reservation in the summer of 1962, my adopted Navajo brothers and I seemed very much alike in one way: with their brown skin, they looked like they did not belong in the white world, even though their every thought told them that they were white; my white skin gave me the appearance of "fitting in" when I reentered the white world, yet my internal voice told me that I belonged to the world of the Navajo.

The story begins in 1958, and in an effort to help you keep track of the names and ages of seven children, I'm going to give you a helping hand. In 1958 the oldest, Marilynn was ten years old. Joellen, next in line was eight, and I was seven. My sister D'Nelle was five, and the youngest, Deanne, was three. In September of 1959 we adopted a Navajo boy, Michael, who was fourteen months old. The following May we adopted another Navajo boy, Daniel, aged eleven months. Michael and Daniel are not related except by adoption. To add to the confusion of names, my parents are named Jo and Joe.

One Navajo legend states that if a coyote crosses your path, you should turn back instead of continuing your journey; to continue would cause bad things to happen. As I look back on my childhood years, it seems as if a coyote crossed my family's path in the summer of 1958—when my father made a decision in anger that changed the course of our lives—but our only choice was to continue on the journey.

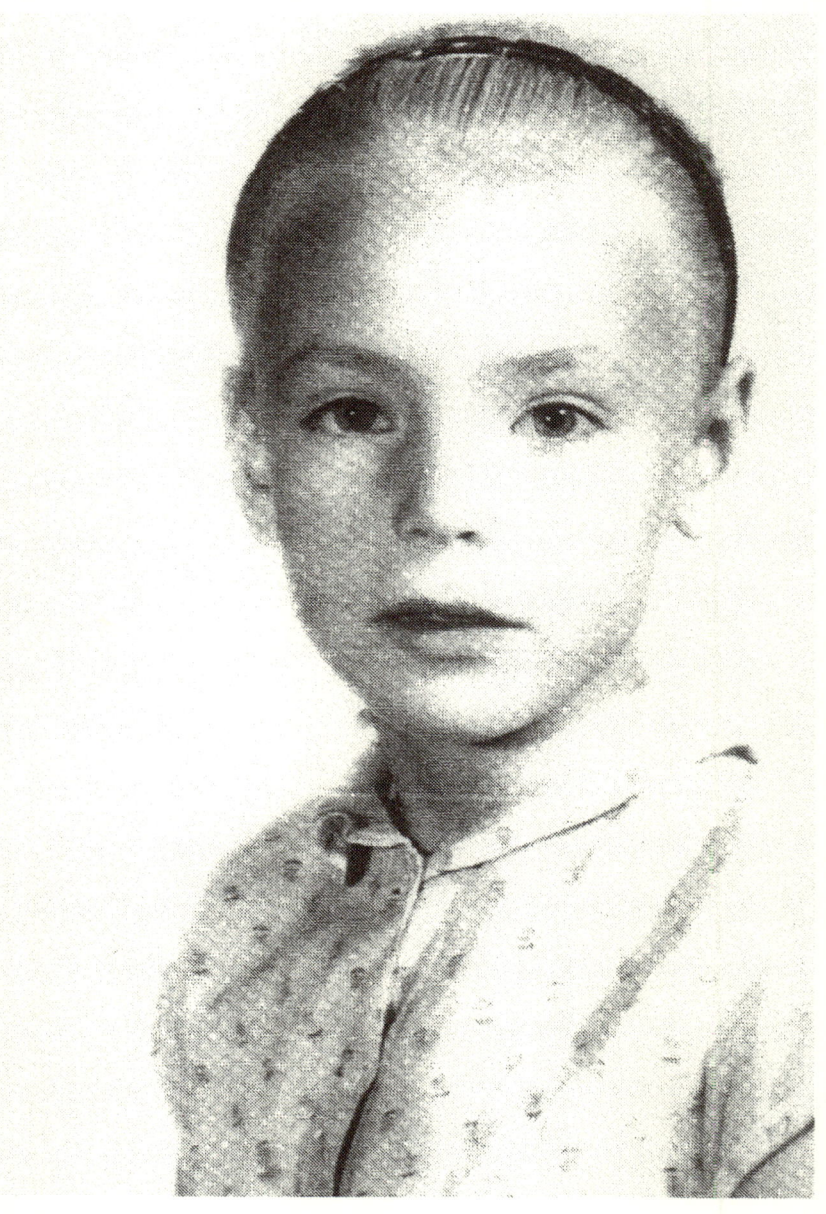

Danalee—age 7

PART I

Navajo Taboo: Do not tell a person to go to hell because it might happen.

○ ○

The United States Supreme Court unanimously rules that Little Rock, Arkansas, schools must integrate.

The Navajo begin a project to pave roads on the reservation.

1

Shiprock, 1958

"Goddamn it! Shut up and get in the car, or I'll leave you and the goddamn dog behind."

Dad's still angry with all of us, especially Mom. Two days ago, he came home from his latest golf tournament trip and had a giant fight with Mom. That afternoon he hitched a U-Haul trailer to the back of the station wagon, loaded it with everything we own, and now we're moving. I don't understand any of it.

My four sisters and I quickly get into the back of the station wagon. "Wait, Dad!" we cry in unison. "Come here, Lady! Come on, girl!"

Dad never says anything he doesn't mean. Lots of times he doesn't speak at all, just to prevent his saying something he doesn't mean. I know he'll drive away and leave our dog behind. I stick my head out of the car window and scream as loudly as I can. "Come *on*, girl! Lady! *Lady!* Come on, girl!"

Dad acts like he has ants in his pants; he can't wait to leave. He looks around the front yard to make sure we haven't left anything and ignores our panicked screams. He slowly walks to the back of the U-Haul trailer and checks the lock. He looks around the side of the house and then ties the last suitcase to the top of the station wagon's roof rack. Dad pokes his head into the car and counts five heads to make sure all of us are in the car. He gets in the driver's side of the car and prepares to drive off without Lady.

Mom hasn't said a word to any of us for the past twenty-four hours; she's turned into a zombie. She's absolutely no help when it comes to saving Lady. She just sits in the passenger seat and stares straight ahead into the glaring late-afternoon sun. Mom's done something horrible, but my sisters and I can't figure out what it is. Not even my oldest sister, Marilynn, who thinks she knows everything, can solve the mystery.

Two days ago Mom and Dad screamed and yelled at each other so loudly that Marilynn made us all get into the bedroom closet while she stood guard by the door. Marilynn said Dad paced back and forth in front of Mom, while Mom sat on the edge of their bed. He screamed at Mom, "Are you a fucking idiot? I don't care if you say nothing happened. You're married, and he asked you to marry him. People will think you're a goddamn whore."

Then, Dad didn't say anything for a long, long time. Finally, Marilynn heard him say, "You can go to hell. I'll take the first fucking job that takes us away from this hellhole of a town."

I guess Dad found a new job because now we're leaving town, but we can't leave without Lady. I hang out of the window and yell one last time, "Come on, Lady!"

Lady rounds the corner of our now-vacant house and jumps through the open window of the car and onto the backseat. Her tongue hangs from her mouth, and her sides heave in and out as if she's run a mile to reach us. My youngest sister, three-year-old Deanne, grabs Lady by the neck and starts stroking her long brown collie hair. Lady pants and licks Deanne's face.

As we drive away from the house, Mom tries once again to talk to Dad. "Please, Joe. Please, let's stay. Nothing happened."

For three days we ride in the hot car—Mom doesn't talk to Dad, and Dad doesn't talk to Mom. They're pretty good at not talking to each other when they are angry. When they aren't talking to each other, they usually aren't talking to us kids, either. For three days Marilynn silently passes out bananas for our snack and peanut butter and jelly sandwiches for breakfast, lunch, and supper. Lady—and everyone else in the car—stinks. Late in the afternoon of the third day, Dad breaks his silence. "We're here."

Dad's last two jobs were at country clubs—he teaches people how to play golf—and before that he coached football at the junior college. Our car stops in front of an old abandoned building. An Indian is standing in front of it, holding his cowboy hat in his hands. He nods to Dad in greeting. Granddad has told me to never talk to "wetbacks" or "injuns," but Dad smiles and shakes hands with the short brown man. Granddad lives in a town where the Mexicans have their own stores and movie theaters, and the white people have their own stores. Granddad likes it that way because then he never has to talk to them.

Dad doesn't seem to mind talking to an Indian. He tells us to get out of the car and wait beside it while he talks to the Indian; he puts Marilynn in charge. Usually, Grandma is in charge. She cooks for us, cleans the house, plays games with us, and babysits when Mom and Dad go to the country club to play golf or bridge.

I don't know who Dad thinks is going to do all of these things, now that Grandma is living in Texas and we are living in this place. Grandma is a better mom than Mom; she knows how to make pancakes and how to wash our clothes, and she knows where the Band-Aids® are if I skin my knee. Granddad would come over whenever Grandma took care of us. Granddad is just like me; he doesn't like to be away from Grandma for very long. I'm not sure where we are now, but Marilynn said that Dad told Mom to go straight to hell, so maybe we're in hell. If Grandma was here, she could tell me if I was in hell.

I'm hot, and ants are crawling on my feet. I want to get back in the car with Mom and Deanne. Mom sits with her door open and her bare feet resting on the edge of the door frame. Deanne wants to stand in line with the rest of us, but Mom has a death grip on her waist. Marilynn, who sometimes thinks she is Mom just because she is the oldest, turns from her lead position in line and reads my mind about wanting to get back into the car.

She stares over my sister Joellen's head and directs her bossy comment to me. "Danalee! If you take one step out of this line I'll grab your skinny little legs and stuff them down that anthill over there."

Marilynn loves being the boss. I try to explain to her why I should get back into the car, but she won't listen to me. She stares down the line at each of us, as if her eyes have the power to keep us in a straight line. She says, "No buts. We'll get of line when Dad tells us we can."

I try another tactic. "You're not the boss of me," I retort. "I don't have to do what you tell me to do."

Marilynn waves her arm in a big circle and asks, "Do you see Grandma anywhere around here? Grandma's not here to protect her precious little goody-two-shoes, so I *am* the boss of you, and you will stay in this line."

D'Nelle, my younger sister who stands behind me, knows better than this. She folds her arms across her five-year-old chest and tells Marilynn, "Mom's the boss of me, not you."

Marilynn shifts her glare from me to D'Nelle. "Mom's a zombie. Do you want a zombie for a boss?"

I shove my older sister Joellen in the back and whisper, "When do I get to be the boss?"

Joellen shrugs her shoulders and whispers back, "How the hell should I know? Just shut up."

D'Nelle seizes on the opportunity to get Joellen in trouble and shouts at the top of her lungs, "Joellen said hell! Joellen said hell!"

Joellen turns around and leans past me so that D'Nelle can see her angry face. She tells D'Nelle through clenched teeth, "Shut the fuck up and stay in line."

D'Nelle continues to holler, "Joellen said hell! Joellen said—"

Marilynn interrupts D'Nelle with a go-to-hell look as she says, "D'Nelle, if you don't stop talking and stay in line I'm gonna stuff you down the anthill right along with Danalee."

Marilynn thinks she's scary, but she never does any of the things she says she's going to do. Once she yelled at Deanne, my three-year-old sister, "Stop being a jabberwocky, or I'll cut out your tongue!" I'm not stupid. I know that Mom and Grandma don't let Marilynn play with knives so she couldn't have cut out Deanne's tongue—although sometimes Deanne talks so much that I'd be perfectly happy if she didn't have a tongue.

Dad is sweating, and his golfing shirt sticks to his back. Dad and the Indian are about the same height, and they both are smoking cigarettes, but the similarity ends there. Dad's tanned skin is not as brown as the Indian's, and their hair is really different. Dad has gray hair—he says he's had gray hair since he was twenty-five years old. The Indian has the thickest and blackest hair I've ever seen. I hope the Indian understands English because Dad seems to be doing most of the talking. The Indian seems to spend more time staring at us than listening to Dad. Dad finally turns and looks at us, too; he calls out to Marilynn, "Oh, for Christ sake, Marilynn. You don't have to keep them in line forever. Everyone can go play."

Dad evidently hasn't looked around—there's no place to play. There's sand, cactus, and ants everywhere. A couple of men dressed in long brown robes wave to us from the porch of a church across the highway, but Mom has told us not to talk to strangers so I don't wave back to them.

Marilynn, Joellen, and I head for the shade of the cottonwood tree that is next to a small house. Marilynn is tall enough to see into the windows of the house, but the windows are all covered with shades so she can't see anything. Joellen ignores the ants and spiders lurking near the cottonwood tree; she lies on the ground under the giant shady tree. I sit in the shade beside her and stare at the buildings around me. Where are all of the people who live in this town? And why is the town surrounded by a metal fence? Maybe a coyote ate them. I saw a coyote just before we arrived. He ran across the road and then stopped right in the middle of the road and stared into our car. Maybe that coyote ate all of the people who live in this town.

D'Nelle makes a beeline for the anthill near the steps of the single-wide mobile home that sits a few feet from the little house. She fills the anthill with sand and watches the ants struggle to get out. Deanne tries to wiggle her way out of Mom's grasp.

When the Indian leaves; Dad stays in the shade of the porch and smokes another cigarette. Dust from the Indian's pickup truck floats in the air above the cattle guard at the entrance to this fenced compound. Dad walks to Mom's side of the car and says, "Come on, Jo. Why don't you go into the house, out of the sun?" He reaches down to help Mom and Deanne out of the car.

Mom jerks her arm away from his hand. "Don't touch me! You're a goddamn jealous idiot to give up your job at the country club to teach school on an Indian reservation. We'll see how well you like it when the Indians show up when school starts." Mom climbs out of the car without Dad's help and hands Deanne to Dad. "Here; take your daughter and put some shoes on her so the ants won't sting her to death. I'm going inside to lie down." Mom walks toward the small house near the cottonwood tree.

Dad calls after her, "We're staying in the mobile home for a while. I need to remodel the little duplex so we can all fit into it. The mobile home has two bedrooms, so the girls can take one of the bedrooms and we'll take the other."

Mom stands perfectly still, as if she were a volcano about to blow her top. Then she changes course and marches over to the mobile home. With her back to Dad she yells, "You can take the couch; I'll take the bedroom!"

When D'Nelle sees Mom coming toward her, she tries to shoo away all of the ants from the top step of the wooden stairs before Mom gets there. Marilynn takes Deanne from Dad's arms and carries her into the mobile home. Mom and Deanne disappear into the back of the mobile home. Marilynn stomps down the steps past D'Nelle and heads to the back of the U-Haul trailer.

Dad mumbles, "Shit." He walks to the car and unties the rope from his old brown suitcase. He lifts it from the top of the car and heads for the single-wide mobile home. When he sees D'Nelle playing with the ants, he hollers, "Leave the fucking anthill alone, and go help your sisters unload the U-Haul!"

Joellen, D'Nelle, and I watch Marilynn pace back and forth behind the U-Haul trailer. She's cursing, "Goddamn new job," "Fucking reservation," and "Shit! Shit!" She's only ten, but she can cuss as good as Dad; she's just lucky that Dad doesn't hear her. Marilynn climbs inside the back of the U-Haul and hands the three of us things to carry to the mobile home.

One look inside the mobile home, and I'm glad that this is only temporary. It's hot, hot, hot and dirty. It takes us the rest of the afternoon to unload the U-Haul. Marilynn and Dad carry the beds and couch and chairs. Joellen and I carry the small maple kitchen table. D'Nelle carries some of the boxes, but at age five she's not strong enough to carry much. It's almost dark by the time Marilynn gets the sheets on our bed and Mom's bed. Dad is going to sleep on the couch.

Our clothes are covered with dust from the unloading. The floor of the mobile home needs to be swept and mopped, the counters need to be cleaned, and the bathroom needs to be scrubbed. Tomorrow will be a long day. We are all exhausted from the afternoon's work.

Mom and Deanne are quiet. Marilynn is in the kitchen, wiping down cabinets. D'Nelle and Dad sit on the old lumpy couch. D'Nelle's small five-year-old body snuggles as close to Dad as she can get; I think that being close to Dad makes her feel less scared. Dad sweats as if he's eaten a jalapeño pepper. Little beads of sweat cling to his crew cut and trickle down the sides of his face. His golf shirt is all dirty from unloading the car and U-Haul. He gently tosses a golf ball from hand to hand and finally breaks his silence. "Girls, Mom isn't feeling well." He stares at the golf ball in his hands. "Marilynn, why don't you make some peanut butter and jelly sandwiches for supper? Joellen, dig through the boxes, and try to find some plates and cups. Danalee, help her. We might as well get settled in."

Marilynn maneuvers fourteen slices of bread onto the tiny kitchen counter and meticulously spreads peanut butter on seven of the slices. The peanut butter is warm and runny from the long ride in the car. I can tell that Marilynn's thinking about something because the skin at the sides of her eyes is crinkled, and she's spreading the peanut butter in slow motion. I think she's working up the nerve to ask Dad a question. Marilynn's the bravest girl I know. Finally, brave Marilynn speaks up. "Dad? Hey, Dad."

Dad is distracted and tired. "What?"

"Are we going to stay in this mobile home while you play in golf tournaments? 'Cause if we are, when's Grandma coming?"

Dad tosses the golf ball faster and faster from one hand to the other. I wonder if he's going to throw it. "I'm not going to play in golf tournaments anymore, and Doris isn't coming to live with us. Your mother can manage without her."

Marilynn's courage continues. "What are you going to do if you don't play golf?"

Dad reaches for his golf bag and unzips the side pocket. He places the small white ball inside and zips the bag closed. "I'm going to teach Indians how to play football and basketball," he says, sounding exhausted. "I'll be a coach and a junior high schoolteacher at the new school that's across the highway. It's the new building next to the Catholic mission." He points out the window in the living room. "The big building you can see on the other side of the split-rail fence is the boarding school for the Navajo children. I don't want you crawling through the fence and going over there. When school starts, you and your sisters will go to the school that's right here in this compound. The boarding school will have about a thousand kids, so just leave them alone and they'll leave you alone."

Marilynn stops spreading grape jelly on the other seven bread slices and glances over at Joellen and me. Like the creamy smooth peanut butter, a smile slowly spreads across her face. I guess she thinks it's a good idea that Dad's going to be around, but I'm not sure. He's usually fun when he's here, but he hasn't been home that much. I'd rather have Grandma come live with us than have Dad home all the time.

Dad continues, "We're just living in the mobile home until I can remodel that little duplex next door—the small house with the big tree beside it. Right now it's a house with two one-bedroom apartments in it, but I'm going to knock out the wall that runs across the middle of the house, and then we'll have two of every-thing: two bedrooms, two living rooms, two kitchens, and two bathrooms. I'll put up a picket fence along one side so your mom will have a yard for Deanne and D'Nelle to play in."

Joellen stops digging through cardboard boxes and yells, "Two bathrooms! I'm going to go tell Mom that we'll have two bathrooms. That'll make her feel better."

I guess it doesn't make Mom feel too much better; she doesn't come out of her new bedroom. She gives Deanne to Joellen and she joins us for supper. After supper my four sisters and I retire to our new bedroom. Dad wedges our double bed into a corner—so that the head of the bed and one side are up against walls—and now we can step into the bedroom without hitting the edge of the bed. We squeeze into the room along the wall that has the closet. With the closet doors open, we take turns standing inside the closet to change into our pajamas. Mari-lynn is the last one into the bed, and she reaches over with her foot and slams the bedroom door shut.

Deanne talks in her sleep. (In fact, Deanne talks all the time—from the moment she wakes up until the moment she falls asleep—kind of like Mom.) It's amazing to me that Deanne can sleep; the tiny room feels like an oven to me. The crank handle of the bedroom's window is missing, so we can't open it. Marilynn's too mad to sleep. Joellen usually can fall asleep anywhere, but tonight she lies on her back and stares at the peeling paint on the ceiling. D'Nelle can't find a space to lie down, so she sits on the bed with her legs curled under her and tries to read in the dark. Like me, she started reading when she was four, and she loves books.

I lie on my back and stare at the spider in the corner of the ceiling and think about my day. The Indian who talked to Dad today seemed nice; he didn't try to scalp me like Granddad said he would. Granddad told me never to talk to Indians, but when school starts I think I will have to talk to some Indians.

The next morning, a silent Mom and Dad take D'Nelle and Deanne with them to Farmington to turn in the U-Haul truck. Farmington is a town off of the reservation, about thirty miles from Shiprock. They'll be gone a while, so Marilynn, Joellen, and I decide to explore the schoolteachers compound. I soon discover that the ground in Shiprock broils under the morning sun and that the metal fence that surrounds our compound will burn your hand if you touch it.

Marilynn, Joellen, and I are the best of buddies, and today we are explorers. We run from the shade of our living room to the shade of the abandoned one-room schoolhouse, just outside the mobile home's front door. The porch of the schoolhouse feels like it is ten degrees cooler than the outside air. From there, we dash across the burning gravel road to the side of the cinder block elementary school. We keep our backs close to cinder block wall and edge our way along the exterior of the building, taking care to stay in the small sliver of shade along the edge of the building.

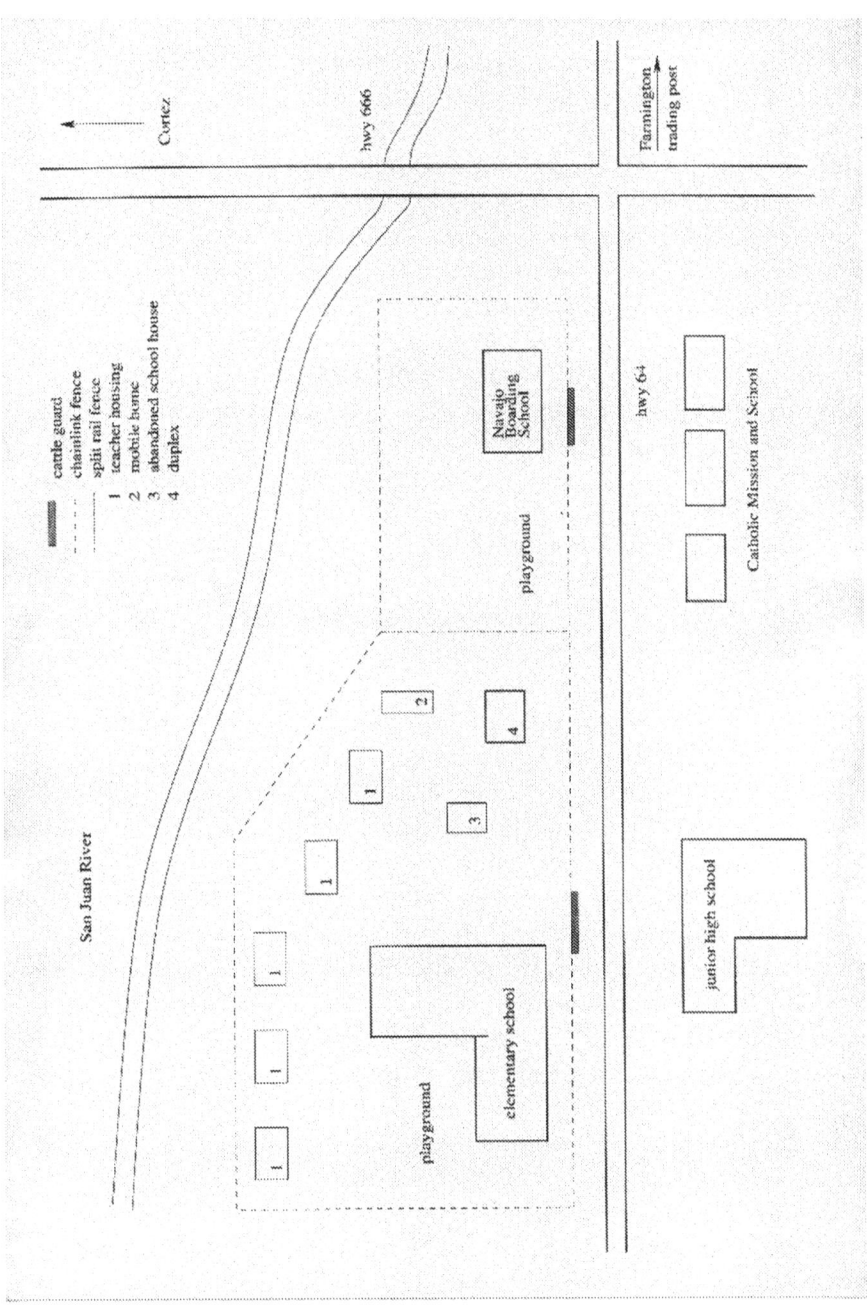

Schoolteacher's Compound

Along the side and at the back of the elementary school, we discover several brown wood-framed houses, but they are all vacant. Everything in Shiprock is brown: the dirt, the elementary school, the Navajo boarding school, the adobe on the duplex, the spiders, and the dusty walls of our bedroom. My elementary school has a small playground with two swings, two teeter-totters, and a tetherball pole, all glaring in the morning's sun. From the back of the elementary school we can see another housing compound on the other side of the metal fence that surrounds the elementary school. Dad told us that the white families who work at the Kerr McGee uranium mine live in this compound. We run to the shade of the last house in our compound and try to peek inside the curtained windows. I wonder when the other schoolteachers will arrive.

Behind the last house in our compound there is a break in the chain-link fence. Marilynn thinks that someone fixed the fence so that you can remove part of it, step through it, and then hook the fence back on the nails so that it looks like it hasn't been moved. Marilynn pulls back on the fence and calls, "Come on, scaredy-cats! Step through the fence."

My eyes concentrate on the blue and green polka dots on Joellen's shorts. I'm sticking close behind her. If a coyote wants to jump out and eat me, I don't want to see him coming. The dirt path rapidly transforms into a cool, moist, leaf-laden path. Within minutes we're walking on soft white puffs of cotton that cover the narrow path. We are in a forest of tall, green cottonwood trees, so numerous and thick that the sun temporarily disappears.

Unaware that Marilynn has stopped, I slam into Joellen's polka dots. An ancient fallen cottonwood tree blocks the path, and it's so large that we can barely see over the top of it. Marilynn, however, announces that she can see the San Juan River in the distance. Far to our right, half of the tree's roots reach for the sky, while the bottom half is hidden in thick black mud. To our left, the trunk of the tree extends beyond our sight. Someone or something has scooped out the dirt under the tree trunk, so we could, if we wanted to, scoot under the trunk and keep exploring. The major flaw with this plan, though, would be in explaining to Dad how we managed to get our clothes muddy. Marilynn offers an alternate plan.

She stands next to the massive tree trunk and issues instructions. "Joellen, cup your hands and lift me up to the top of the trunk. Danalee, cup your hands for Joellen so she can get over the trunk, and then the two of us will lift you up."

Marilynn is so smart. The plan works flawlessly. On the other side of the trunk, a gray boulder provides a step from which Marilynn and Joellen jump to the ground and continue their explorations. I lie on my back on the smooth-barked tree and stare at the wonders around me. Clouds shade me from the intense heat of the sun. A row of giant cottonwood trees, clumped together like best friends, line the path, green leaves quiver in a light breeze. Birds chatter and fly up and down the path, unsure of whom they should watch—my sisters or me.

I sit on the edge of the tree and dangle my legs over the side. From the top of the trunk, I, too, can see the slow-moving San Juan River. Maybe the path leads to the river, but from my perspective it looks like I'd have to make my way along a path that's overgrown with shrubs; thick, brown cattails; green, marshy reeds; and black mud. I'd much rather stay on top of my tree trunk and watch the clouds play hide-and-seek with the sun.

Before we head home, Marilynn, Joellen, and I spit into the palms of our hands and then shake hands. We swear not to tell a living soul about the break in the fence because now, the fallen cottonwood tree will be our secret hideout.

The hot summer days all seem to melt into one. Each morning before I get out of bed, I can hear mice trying to get to the kitchen before Dad does, mourning doves beginning their chorus of coos, and horseflies crashing into the bedroom window screen.

I lie on my back in our crowded bed and stare at the flaky, peeling paint on the ceiling. I remember what it felt like to wake up at Grandma's house when I spent the night with her. The scent of hot muffins would fill my bedroom, and Grandma's voice would call me to breakfast. I wish she was here or that I was there. I can't remember a time in which Grandma didn't take care of me.

I miss Granddad and the way he would sneak up behind me and hug me, asking, "How's my little shit this morning?" And Grandma would scold him: "Now, Skeet, don't call our angel a little shit." I wish they were here; Mom is always happy when her mom is near.

I watch the sunlight sneak around the corners of the dirty bedroom curtains and splash against the wall. I hear Lady slurp water from her bowl on the kitchen floor. Dad's cigarette smoke seeps under our closed bedroom door.

When Dad gets up off the living room couch, he whirls through the tiny kitchen like a small tornado. Bowls slam against the Formica countertop. Spoons crash to the linoleum floor. The refrigerator door opens and then slams shut five or six times, as if he can't remember to grab the bottle of milk the first time he opens the refrigerator door. He's still too mad to be quiet.

Mom has resumed her position of refusing to leave the back bedroom, except to go to the bathroom or to cook french fries for herself. Mom loves french fries and Coca-Cola; she makes the best french fries. She scrubs the skin of the potato and then slices it into thin rounds. While she's slicing, the oil in the cast-iron skillet is heating, and when it's just right she carefully drops the potatoes in and stirs them. When the potatoes are fried, she mixes catsup and mayonnaise together and spreads it over the top of her potatoes. Since we moved to Shiprock, she hasn't shared her fries with us. She takes her potatoes and Coke into her back bedroom and slams the door. Marilynn's not allowed to heat the oil, so she can't make fries us, and Grandma's not here to do it, so we don't get any french fries.

Like a broken record, each morning Mom yells at Dad to fix breakfast for us, but Marilynn has already done it. Around noon, Mom yells at Dad to fix lunch for us, but Marilynn has already done that, too. If Marilynn could drive a car, she'd drive to Farmington and buy some groceries for us. Dad seems to be engaged in a waiting contest with Mom to see who's going to buy groceries first. I know that Mom will not be first, because she told me that she's afraid of injuns and coyotes and spiders.

Today Marilynn, Joellen, and I sit in the shade of the porch of the abandoned schoolhouse. We see a woman cross over the cattle guard. She wears cotton trousers, with a big, shiny concho belt wrapped around her small waist. Her worn cowboy boots look like my granddad's. She stops in front of us, pushes back her stained cowboy hat, and grins from ear to ear. "Morning, y'all. Is your ma about?"

Marilynn runs into the mobile home to retrieve Mom from the back bedroom, and Joellen and I follow with the woman, who tells us that her name is Vicky and that she lives at the trading post. We show her into the living room, and Deanne and D'Nelle stare at her from the hallway. Mom, hair combed and wearing a clean blouse, rushes down the hall to meet her guest. Vicky is delighted to meet all of us, but says that she was hoping for some boys to play with her two boys, rather than five girls. Vicky invites Mom to walk up to the trading post some day for a visit. Marilynn informs her that Mom is afraid to leave the mobile home. Vicky laughs really loud, like a snorting pig, and tells Mom that there is no reason to be afraid of the Navajo. Vicky's lived in Shiprock all her life, and so has her husband, Jim. She knows a lot about Shiprock and the Navajo.

She accepts Mom's offer of a cold Coca-Cola and settles onto the lumpy couch to tell us a little about the Navajo. She begins with the story of how the Navajo came to Shiprock: "According to Navajo creation stories, the Navajo moved through a series of worlds before reaching their current fourth world. In each previous world, they somehow displeased the gods and had to flee to the next world. The town of Shiprock is named for the rock formation that resembles a sailing ship—it's over seven thousand feet tall.

"The Navajo call the rock *Tse'Bit 'ai,* or the "Rock with Wings," because it carried the people to safety a long time ago. According to Navajo legend, after the Navajo had lived here a while, a pair of fierce gigantic creatures called *Tse' na'hale* came and lived on *Tse'Bit 'ai.*" Vicky leans down closer to Deanne's frightened face and says, "The *Tse' na'hale* were very, very mean; they caught and devoured people." Then Vicky smiles and tells us, "A young warrior named Monster Slayer killed them with his lightning arrow and saved the people."

My sisters and I listen to Vicky's every word; we don't want her to leave. Vicky seems to love to talk. She tells us another story, one of the sacred mountains that surround the reservation.

"The Navajo believe that long, long ago, even before the time of Monster Slayer, First Man and First Woman created the first hogan, a home for the Navajo. They also created the earth's land formations, including the four sacred mountains. The four mountains have a special meaning to the Navajo, and white people aren't supposed to go there." She smiles again. "The more you know about the Navajo, the less you'll be afraid. All Navajo children know about the sacred mountains, so we should also learn their names. The sacred mountain to the north is Mount Hesperus, or *Dibé Nitsaa;* to the east is Mount Blanca, or *Tsi-snaasjini';* to the south is Mount Taylor, or *Tsoodzil;* and to the west is the San Francisco Peaks, or *Doko' oosliid.*"

I don't think I'll ever learn how to pronounce the Navajo words, but I think I can remember Hesperus, Blanca, Taylor, and San Francisco. Vicky is a great storyteller. Before she leaves she again invites Mom to walk up the highway to the trading post. Then she gives each of us a tiny piece of turquoise, because according to Navajo legend, turquoise is good luck. I stick the small rock into the pocket of my shorts and wait for some good luck to happen.

It takes about a week for the turquoise's good luck to happen.

It's a scorching afternoon, and Mom floats out of her bedroom, wearing her light blue dress that she wears to the country club. She's hardly come out of her room for weeks, and now she's all dressed up as if she's going to church. Her auburn hair is hidden under the wide brim of a straw hat. A small clutch purse appears to be glued to her right palm. Her dress floats around her shins and the new hose she bought before we left Texas. When she isn't crying, I have the prettiest mom.

She stands in the middle of the living room, careful not to let her dress touch the dusty coffee table, and says in a strong, Grandma-like voice, "Marilynn, I want you to babysit D'Nelle and Deanne while Joellen and Danalee and I walk to the trading post. We're going to visit Vicky and pick up a few things."

I see the shock on Marilynn's face; she can't believe she's being left behind. "But Mom, that's not fair," she complains. "I'm the oldest. I should get to walk to the trading post. Joellen can babysit."

"You'll do what I ask you to do," Mom snaps. "You can go another day. Joellen and Danalee, put on a dress and comb your hair. We might be living with Indians, but you don't have to look like them."

I think about volunteering to babysit rather than comb my hair. I have a giant snarled knot at the back of my head. I can't reach it with my brush, and I'm not about to ask Marilynn to help me. I gently comb a thin layer of hair over the knot and Joellen and I join Mom in the living room. We step into the bright afternoon sunshine and hotfoot our way across the metal beams of the cattle guard. The high chain-link fence that surrounds the elementary school glistens in the sun.

Joellen and I surreptitiously wave to Dad, who is working on the conversion of the duplex. He wants to finish the project before school starts. He stops hammering and stares in disbelief at the three of us. I twirl around so he can see my new dress. Mom doesn't look at him. She holds my hand so tight it hurts; she's gripping Joellen's hand, too. She's trying to not be afraid of Indians. I know she's watched from her bedroom window as some of the Navajo herd their sheep down the middle of the highway, but I think she's still a little afraid of actually meeting one. Mom keeps to the edge of the asphalt as we walk toward the trading post. The Catholic mission is directly across from the duplex, and she wants to avoid Brother Frank, the man who waved to us on our first day here.

Brother Frank stops sweeping the porch of the Catholic church to wave to us. Mom nods politely but doesn't stop to chat. Joellen and I wave to Brother Frank and smile. He stopped by the mobile home shortly after we arrived and told us all about himself and his church. There's a school at the church, and he was disappointed to discover that we are not Catholic. He politely pointed out that members of the Methodist church have services at the junior high school each week and that there is also a Baptist church and a Presbyterian church in town. I have never been to church, so learning that there are so many churches in Shiprock makes me a little nervous, I might have to go to one of them. Like Vicky, Brother Frank has a happy smile and isn't afraid of the Navajo. He told Mom and Dad that he's never met a kinder, gentler people.

The old Catholic church has been in Shiprock almost as long as the trading post. Made from adobe bricks, the church is cool in the summer and warm in the winter. One end of the church has a large cafeteria that Brother Frank turns into a roller-skating rink in the summer. Brother Frank always wears a long brown robe with a rope wrapped around his waist, like a belt. I've never seen anyone dress like that. His hair is cut even shorter than Dad's crew cut.

I've heard Dad call Brother Frank a "fucking holy roller." Brother Frank told us that the families whose dads work at the uranium mine, which is thirty miles from Shiprock, live in the housing compound on the other side of our chain-link fence. The compound is called the Kerr-McGee housing compound because that's the name of the company that owns the uranium mine. I smile and don't tell him that I already know that. When school starts, all of the white kids who live in that compound will go to my school. There is a break in the fence with a stile that allows the kids to cross over into the schoolteachers compound. Mom is reassured to know that there are white people living next to us.

After we pass the Catholic mission I get a good look at the new junior high school, where Dad will coach when school starts. As far back as I can remember, Dad's never worked inside a building. He's played golf for a living and coached junior college football, both outside activities. I wonder how he'll like being inside a classroom with a bunch of junior high school students all day. I know he liked playing golf. When we lived in Del Rio, Texas, he liked golf so much that we hardly ever saw him—although he did build my sisters and me our own play-house in our backyard in Del Rio. Our yard overflowed with orange trees, and Dad built the little white playhouse—complete with three windows and a door—behind the orange grove. The playhouse was much more fun to play in than the porch of the abandoned schoolhouse.

Dad's said that the trading post is the liveliest spot in town; he's already been there several times. As we approach it, I think the patched-together wooden building looks like it might fall over at any moment. Wide wooden steps lead to the heavy, wooden front door. The scent of leather, wool, stale coffee, and unwashed bodies greets us as we walk into the trading post. I hold my breath when a Navajo passes. The Navajo men smell like they never take a bath!

I used to love bath time, but now I hate it. Mom and Dad are careful with the water we use because there's not a lot of water in our well. We only get one bath a week, and it's not like when I took a bath in Texas, when I could stay in the tub by myself for a long time. Now bath time means a tub half filled with water. Deanne and D'Nelle go first, and Mom makes them get in and out real fast. Then Joellen and I get in the same water and get wet all over, and when we get out, Marilynn gets into the same water by herself, but she never stays in very long.

I look around the trading post. Beautiful dolls stand at attention on a wooden shelf along one wall. Navajo rugs hang from ceiling beams. Wrinkled leather harnesses and saddles occupy the floor. Unpolished turquoise and sparkling, shiny silver jewelry lay in a glass display case. I stare at the leather moccasins that hang from pegs on the wall behind the cash register. I'd give anything for a pair of moccasins.

Joellen and I quickly sidestep Mom and run to Vicky to say hi. She introduces us to her husband, Jim. Vicky wears the same clothes she wore when she visited us. Her black hair is cut short and looks like she cut it herself. Her dancing eyes make us smile. Joellen and I roam the large room,

We hide behind the saddles and watch Mom collect her letters from Grandma and her latest Sears and Roebuck catalog. She caresses a cold bottle of Coca-Cola as she stands next to the glass jewelry case and pretends to look at its contents. She casually sips her Coke and slyly watches the Navajo men and women who are in the trading post today. Mom is trying to get over her fear of Indians.

The Navajo men wear sweat-rimmed cowboy hats and plaid shirts, faded jeans, and worn and dusty cowboy boots. I wish my hair was long enough to wear in a bun at the base of my neck like the Navajo men and women wear theirs.

Joellen whispers in my ear, "I bet Mom would like to have one of those purple blouses."

I whisper back, "I'd rather have a long velvet skirt but only if I can also have some moccasins and all the silver jewelry on that lady's arm."

The Navajo women who stand at the counter and talk with Vicky wear silver necklaces tightly around their necks, as well as longer necklaces made of turquoise and silver that dangle down their fronts. Silver bracelets hug their wrists. The Navajo women wear the most beautiful clothes I've ever seen—satin purple blouses and red velveteen skirts.

Vicky joins Mom at the jewelry case and teaches Mom how to say hello in Navajo (ya'at'eeh), and as we leave the trading post to walk home, Mom nods her head to a Navajo woman entering the trading post and says ya'at'eeh. She smiles to herself at her newfound courage.

The next day Marilynn sits on top of the plywood garbage can tower that is outside, next to the back of the duplex, and throws rocks at Joellen and me. She's still mad at us for going to the trading post. The plywood garbage can tower keeps the two dented metal garbage cans off of the ground and away from coyotes. The thought that a coyote could come so close to my house is scary.

Joellen and I use the garbage can tower to spy on the Navajo men who work on the boarding school's playground. The boarding-school kids will be showing up soon, so the men are greasing the merry-go-round and putting a new chain on the tetherball pole and new wooden seats on the swings. We've already played on the equipment on our school's playground and sneaked into the marshy area behind the fence that Dad made off-limits to us, but we can't take our eyes off of the tall metal slide on the boarding school's playground. Dad also gave us strict orders to stay off the boarding school's playground, but Joellen and I are working on a plan to play on that slide.

We've lived on the reservation for about a month now, which means that Dad hasn't played golf in about a month. He solves his lack-of-golf problem and our desire to play on the slide at the boarding school by devising a way to play golf in the desert. His desert "golf course" doesn't have a long green fairway, but it does have lots of sand for sand traps. It doesn't have a putting green, but it does have a small patch of grass in the side yard of the duplex, where Dad can stand and hit golf balls onto the playground of the boarding school.

His plan calls for Marilynn, Joellen, and me to climb the split-rail fence and stand on the boarding school's playground. He then will stand near our remodeled duplex and hit a bucket of balls our direction. We need to stay out of sight while he's hitting the balls and then when he's finished, we are to pick them all up so he can start over again.

Dad pulls on his golf glove. He dumps a bucket of balls onto the ground and hands the empty bucket to Marilynn. Marilynn, Joellen, and I climb through the split-rail fence and run to the boarding school's playground. Our first job is to seek shelter before Dad starts hitting the balls.

Marilynn quickly stands by the tetherball pole and makes sure Joellen and I have the right protection. She yells in a frustrated voice, "Danalee, get your head under that slide! If one of those balls hits you in the head, you'll be dumber than you already are!" She watches Joellen trying to climb on top of the teeter-totter and grumbles, "That goes for you, too, Joellen. Get underneath the teeter-totter, not on top of it. How dumb can you get?"

Joellen looks at Marilynn standing by the tetherball pole. "How come you're not under something? Are you dumb?" she snaps.

Before Dad hits the first ball, I crouch under the curved section of the tall metal slide and plug my ears with my fingers. Golf balls hitting metal make a lot of noise. Joellen covers her head with her hands and closes her eyes. Marilynn bravely aligns her slender body with the metal pole of the tetherball. "Dad won't hit me," she says. "Watch your heads; here they come!"

A series of small white balls bounce off the dry, cracked ground. Some disappear under fallen cottonwood leaves, and others roll under the motionless merry-go-round or get snarled in tumbleweeds. Some balls bounce into the cool shade of the adobe building.

Marilynn smiles. "It's okay now, chickens. Come on out and start picking up balls."

I grab the empty bucket and start collecting golf balls. Dad knows exactly how many balls he's hit, and he expects that number retuned to him. Marilynn carries the heavy bucket back to Dad, and Joellen and I finally get to slide down the tallest slide in the world.

Dad hits golf balls every Sunday until a week before school starts. That's when Marilynn gets sick, and golf is the last thing we are thinking about. All of Mom's hard work to learn to like the Navajo and her new life on the reservation and not being mad at Dad and letting him share her bedroom now comes crashing down on Dad's head. When we first arrived on the reservation Brother Frank warned Mom and Dad to make sure none of us got sick.

He told us that Navajo children die every year of rheumatic fever and scarlet fever, measles, and mumps. There is a small, poorly staffed hospital in Shiprock, but most of Brother Frank's parishioners come to him for help—the Navajo believe that a hospital in a house of death because from their perspective, people who go there usually die there.

Marilynn has a high temperature for four days. Without Grandma around to tell Mom what to do, Mom doesn't know how to help Marilynn. When Marilynn's arms and legs begin to swell on the fifth day of her illness, Mom finally sends Dad to fetch Brother Frank. We are supposed to be in bed but my sisters and I can't sleep, we worry about Marilynn.

Joellen, D'Nelle, and Deanne hide behind me in the dark narrow hallway of the mobile home. My sisters and I all smell like sweat. Tears run unstopped down our faces. Marilynn lies on the living room couch, and we want to see her, but we don't want Mom or Dad to see us because we were told to stay in our room. I can see everyone in the living room, even Lady, who's lying beside the couch, but I can't hear what they are saying. I need to get closer.

Like the Navajo women in their long skirts, Brother Frank never seems to sweat in his long brown robe. It covers the floor and the arm of the couch when he leans over to check Marilynn's temperature. The lumpy couch sags under the weight of Mom and Marilynn. The dim light from the dirty overhead fixture casts eerier shadows on Mom's face. Mom sits on the couch with Marilynn's head in her lap. Dad hovers nearby. Brother Frank kneels beside Marilynn and shakes the thermometer hard enough to break it. Then he says something to Mom and Dad in a voice so quiet that I can't hear him. When Brother Frank is through talking, Mom glares at Dad and cries, "You killed her! You brought us to this hellhole and killed her!"

Joellen, standing behind me, shoves me in the back and whispers in a panicked voice, "Is she dead? Can you see her?"

I don't know how to answer her. Marilynn looks like she might be dead, but if she is, why is Brother Frank checking her temperature? I turn and whisper to Joellen, "I don't think so. I'm going to get a little closer. I'll be back in a minute. You guys stay right here and for god's sake, be quiet."

D'Nelle doesn't know how to be quiet. "When is it my turn to be the lookout? I want a turn."

Joellen stops her from running ahead of me, and I whisper to her, "Get back in the bedroom. You don't want Dad to see you. I'll be right back."

I silently creep down the darkened hallway; my eyes focus on the couch. Mom is stroking Marilynn's sweat-drenched, limp hair. Her frantic eyes dart from Brother Frank to Dad to Marilynn. Brother Frank is talking again.

I listen to what he says and then tiptoe back to the dark bedroom to make my report. "Brother Frank says Dad needs to drive Marilynn to Cortez. It'll take about an hour, but they have a hospital there where white people can go. He says she needs to get there as fast as Dad can drive. Mom is still crying; she keeps mumbling that Dad killed Marilynn, but I don't think she's dead. I saw her move."

Before they leave for the hospital, Mom comes to our bedroom. She kneels down and hugs Joellen and me to her side. "I want you two to be my big helpers for Brother Frank. Your Dad and I are going to drive Marilynn to Cortez, and I don't know how long we'll be there."

Through her tears Joellen asks, "Is Marilynn going to die?"

Mom shakes her head back and forth. "I don't know. She's very sick."

I wonder what made her so sick and ask, "What's romantic fever?"

Mom stands up. "It's *rheumatic* fever, not romantic fever, and I guess there's a lot of it on the reservation. It makes you really sick for a long time."

Joellen asks, "But Mom, how come Marilynn can't just go the hospital down the street?"

Mom is anxious to leave but takes the time to answer Joellen. "That hospital is only for the Navajo. White people can't go there. We'll be back as soon as we can. I will call Skeet and Doris, and they'll be here in a few days. Brother Frank will take care of you until they arrive."

I try to keep the sound of hope out of my voice. "Are Grandma and Grandpa going to live with us now?"

Mom gives each of us a kiss. "They'll stay with us in Shiprock until I get home from the hospital in Cortez, and then they're going to live in Farmington, the town where we drive to buy groceries. You'll see them every day until Marilynn is better. Now, the two of you are in charge until your grandparents arrive. You have to help Brother Frank take care of D'Nelle and Deanne, and you have to take care of the house while I'm gone."

After they leave, I lie awake and listen to D'Nelle cry. She hardly ever lets anyone see her cry, but I can always hear her.

The next morning, I hear the mice in the kitchen, as usual. I hear Lady push her empty water bowl across the kitchen floor—I suppose she's wondering when Dad will wake up and give her some water. I climb across Joellen's sleeping body and quietly walk to the kitchen. I'm afraid for Marilynn. Sometimes she's really mean, but I don't want her to die.

Marilynn—1958

2

School Days

Brother Frank arrives bright and early to collect D'Nelle and Deanne and take them across the highway to the Catholic mission for the day. Five-year-old D'Nelle stands in front of Brother Frank with her hands on her hips and yells, "Piss off!"

Joellen, the new boss, corrects her sister in her best Marilynn imitation. "You can't tell Brother Frank to piss off. Now, hold on to his hand so he can take you across the highway to the church, and don't be a pest."

D'Nelle jumps on the lumpy couch and ignores Joellen. She playfully yells, "Piss off!"

Joellen stomps her foot. "Stop it!"

D'Nelle spins around and around and yells at the top of her lungs, "Piss off! Piss off! Piss off!"

Three-year-old Deanne twirls around, saying, "Holy moly! Holy moly!"

I can't believe they are acting like this. I yell at them. "Stop it right now!"

D'Nelle stops spinning and shoves Joellen in the chest when Joellen tries to lift her off of the couch. D'Nelle says, "You can piss off, too. I'm not going with Brother Frank. I'm a helper like you."

Brother Frank grabs the chatterboxes by their hands and drags their wiggly bodies across the cattle guard and toward the church. He turns and hollers over his shoulder, "It's all right, girls. I don't mind if they call me names. We'll be back for lunch, and you'll need to stay in the mobile home with them while they nap. Let's meet in your living room at noon."

Joellen and I spend the next hour cleaning the house and trying to be Mom's helpers. We do the breakfast dishes, clean the bathroom, make the beds, and dust the living room furniture. The interior of the mobile home has reached ninety degrees by the time we finish being helpers. We are both worried about Marilynn but know we won't hear from Mom or Dad until late tonight, when they said they'd call Brother Frank to let him know what's happening. We climb the split-rail fence and slide on the slide until it's time to head back for lunch.

On our way back to the mobile home, we decide to explore the grove of cottonwood trees that are closest to the duplex but still on the grounds of the boarding school. We find a trapdoor in the ground under one of the cottonwood trees. We only found it because Joellen stumped her big toe on the hidden handle of the door. When we lift the door, cool underground air escapes. We climb down into the dark space and discover a small room, about four feet by four feet. Someone has dug tiny shelves out of the dirt walls and even formed a bench in the wall, where we sit and survey the space. The room is deep enough for me to stand up if I hunch over a bit. I wonder what game the school kids play in a cool, dark hole in the ground. Maybe they just climb down in the hole to get out of the heat. We leave everything just as we found it and run to the mobile home to fix peanut butter and jelly sandwiches for D'Nelle and Deanne.

Three days later, Joellen and I are standing in the middle of the highway, watching for Granddad's 1953 white Buick. He and Grandma are to arrive today, and I want to be the first one to hug Grandma; Joellen plans to beat me to it. Grandma is going to take care of us while Mom is away, just like old times.

Joellen and I stand back-to-back, watching in both directions of the highway. We need to pee, but neither one of us wants to leave the highway. I suggest to Joellen that she run to the bathroom first while I keep waiting, but Joellen's no dummy; she's going to stand right here so she can hug Grandma first. I realize we don't have to argue. "Wait a minute," I tell her. "There are two bathrooms in the duplex. Let's run in there and both go at the same time and then run back here."

We run as fast as our loaded bladders will allow. I hear the car bump across the cattle guard as we flush the toilets. Granddad is pulling in next to the mobile home when we burst from the duplex and make a beeline for Grandma's short, sturdy body. We hit her full force as she steps from the car.

She leans down and hugs us both. She says in her soft voice, "Hey, my two sweethearts. You don't need to cry. I'm here now. It will be all right."

The time I spent without Grandma made me feel like I was taking half breaths, but now, with her standing in front of me, I can breathe again. Grandma looks just the same as the last time I saw her—uncombed brown hair, pointy-framed glasses, and an old floppy hat that hangs from a string down her back. She wears baggy blue jeans with a plaid shirt tucked inside of them. Her worn tennis shoes look like they'll fall apart at any moment. She holds a Lucky Strike cigarette between her fingers but far away from us when she hugs us.

Granddad, who could be Grandma's twin with a cigarette balanced between his fingers and dressed like Grandma, except that he's six foot five, and she's five feet tall, sneaks up behind me, picks me up and twirls me around and gives me a big hug. He whispers in my ear, "How's my little shit doing? You miss me? I sure missed you and your sisters."

Granddad's a skinny giant with no teeth and wrinkled skin. He puts me down and lifts Joellen high in air and hugs her. He looks around and says, "Where are those two little pipsqueaks you call sisters?"

D'Nelle and Deanne run ahead of a scurrying Brother Frank, who is bringing them back from the mission, and each of them grab one of Granddad's skinny legs. They say over and over again, "Grandpa! Grandpa!"

Grandma picks up each of them and gives them a hug. I stand to the side and watch. I'm so happy Grandma is here; I know everything will be all right.

A few days later, Joellen and I are once again standing in the middle of the highway; this time we're waiting for Dad. The smell of sheep dung that is splattered across the highway, overpowers me, and horseflies take turns pounding into my shoulder. Dad's driving home from Cortez today, and I'm afraid he's going to be mad when he gets here because Granddad's been fooling around with Dad's remodeling project.

Last night as I lay in bed, I thought of all of the changes to the schoolteachers compound that have happened since Dad drove Marilynn to the hospital a week ago. Two new kids and their parents arrived yesterday, but Granddad called them half-breeds and said we couldn't play with them, even though they are the same age as Marilynn and Joellen. A really, really old lady with white hair moved into one of the houses behind the elementary school. She's one of the schoolteachers, and her husband just sits on their porch all day and won't even say hi to us.

This morning a family arrived with two more kids about my age, but Granddad won't let me talk to them because they are German. Seems like Granddad only likes to talk to white people, like us. He's told me not to talk to Indians, Mexicans, half-breeds, and now Germans. Yesterday when Granddad was hammering in the duplex and talking to himself, I heard him call Dad a "goddamn cradle robber," but I know Dad's never stolen anything. I do know that Dad's going to be mad as hell when he finds out Granddad has been working on the duplex.

When Dad sees Joellen and me standing in the middle of the highway, he honks his horn and waves. Joellen and I skip across the cattle guard and follow the car to the mobile home. Granddad emerges from the duplex, holding a hammer. He nods his head to Dad. Joellen and I decide to wait before running up to hug Dad. His face has turned kind of red, and he's fixated on the hammer in Granddad's hand.

Granddad asks, "How are Marilynn and Jo Eva doing? I'm surprised you didn't kill them all, moving them to this hellhole."

Dad doesn't waver from Granddad's glare. He finally says, "They are doing fine. Jo Eva says to say hi." Dad pauses for a moment and then reaches over and takes the hammer from Granddad. "I'll take care of remodeling the duplex. I don't need your help." He then turns to us and gives us one of his best big smiles—the smile where the sides of his face get deep wrinkles, and I can see all of his teeth, and his eyes turn the color of the sky. He reaches down and gives us a big hug. "How are you two doing? You did a good job of holding down the fort. Come on, girls. I smell something cooking. Is Doris making one of her special suppers for us?"

The next day Dad resumes his work on the duplex. Granddad leaves early and drives to Farmington to check on his new job, which is driving a Texaco gasoline truck, and to find a place for him and Grandma to live. I want them to live with us, but I don't know where they'd sleep. Dad surprises us all at lunchtime when he announces we will move into the duplex tomorrow.

Like all of the days so far in Shiprock, it's boiling hot on the day we move from the mobile home into the remodeled duplex. Dad, with his arms full of boxes, chides me, "Come on, Danalee, stop complaining, and just carry the fucking boxes over to the house. All of the boxes with a red X go in the kitchen. Doris is waiting for you. When you're finished with those, you and Joellen can carry your things over to your new bedroom." He calls over his shoulder as he walks toward the duplex. "Marilynn says if you break anything that belongs to her, she'll wring your neck."

An hour later, I stumble into my new bedroom and dump an armful of clothes onto the foot of my bed. I sort through the pile to find my own things and toss Marilynn's across the room onto her bed. In our new bedroom, Joellen and I will share a double bed, and Marilynn gets her own twin bed. Joellen and I have stuffed Marilynn's little bed in the corner, as far away from our bed as we can push it.

D'Nelle and Deanne also have their own beds in the room across from our bedroom. Dad removed the central wall of the duplex, so Deanne and D'Nelle now have a bedroom that once was a kitchen. Marilynn, Joellen, and I have one of the original bedrooms, and the other bedroom is at the opposite end of the house—that one is for Mom and Dad. Our room has one window and old hard-wood floors that are scratched and marred from past residents, but we don't care.

We're in the first room inside the house, and the exterior door faces the elementary school, so we'll never be late for school.

From the room across from mine, I hear D'Nelle whine, "I hate this room. I want to be in Danalee's room. I don't want a kitchen for a bedroom."

Joellen tries to reassure her. "But Dad made bunk beds for you and Deanne. You get to sleep on the top bunk. You can put everything up there that you don't want Deanne to touch. Come on; let's climb to the top."

In D'Nelle and Deanne's kitchen-bedroom, Dad took all of the cabinets off of the walls and covered the sink and stove top with a piece of plywood. The lower kitchen cabinets now hold D'Nelle's and Deanne's clothes. Their room is only six feet wide, kind of like the interior of a train car. On the side of the kitchen where the small kitchen table used to be, Dad built the girls a set of bunk beds with railings and painted them bright green.

I sneak past the room so D'Nelle won't see me and set off to examine the rest of my new house. As Dad promised, there are two bathrooms. Having two toilets is the best part of this house! Outside the bathrooms, Dad made room for Mom's washer and dryer. We only use the dryer in the wintertime. Hanging clothes on the line outside is one of my favorite chores.

On the other side of the hallway from Mom and Dad's bedroom is the living room/dining room, made from the two living rooms in the original duplex, the big room has beat-up hardwood floors and two small windows. I wish we could afford one of the Navajo rugs from the trading post for our floor. Granddad, with his arms full of one of our living room chairs, sees me standing around doing nothing. "Hey, little shit," he calls to me, "get over to the mobile home and get some more boxes."

The duplex house is much nicer to live in than the mobile home was, and when Mom comes home from Cortez she says she loves the new kitchen and big living room. Mom decides to call the door that is closest to my bedroom the "front door"; the door that is closest to the boarding school is the "back door." She drives to Cortez three times a week to see Marilynn, and Dad drives two times a week. On the days when Mom is at home, Grandma teaches her how to cook.

Mom can now make macaroni and cheese and French toast. It's great having Grandma live close to us again. I go and stay with her in Farmington when Granddad is away for two or three days, driving the gasoline truck around New Mexico.

Lately, Dad has been busy getting ready for the first day of school, like all of the other schoolteachers who live in the compound. I'm busy getting ready for the Navajo kids to arrive at the boarding school. Granddad teases me that I'd better watch out for my scalp, but I've been around the Navajo at the trading post long enough to know that no one is going to scalp me. Vicky tells me that there will be lots of Navajo kids in my classroom but so far, I haven't seen any Navajo kids, only adults. The schoolteachers and the Kerr-McGee compounds only have white kids. I have no idea where the Navajo kids live, but Vicky says they live on ranches around Shiprock or in new houses along the highway. They must never get to walk to the trading post with their moms, like me, because I have never seen them.

The best place to watch the Navajo kids arrive at the boarding school is at the top of the garbage can tower. From there I can easily see the buses arrive, and I can even hear the teachers talking. The first yellow school bus arrives by 8:00 AM, and the children who get off the bus stand at attention in a straight, silent line. The older children hold the hands of the younger ones. Two Navajo women, who are dressed like white women instead of in the traditional Navajo clothing, welcome the kids and then explain the boarding school's rules. They speak in English the whole time, just like Vicky said they would.

It looks like some of the older Navajo kids are translating the women's words for the younger kids, who don't speak English yet. The Navajo women wait patiently while the older kids explain things. My feet dangle from the plywood tower. My eyes are glued to the scene taking place in front of the boarding school. The Navajo boys wear turquoise bracelets, and the girls have on beautiful silver concho belts and long, colorful skirts. I'm so jealous; everyone who gets off the bus is wearing moccasins. I want some moccasins.

I like their shiny black hair—it's pulled back into tight buns at the base of their necks. Each child stands silently in the hot sun and listens as the women talk. After a few minutes, one of the Navajo women walks slowly down the line of children and collects each child's turquoise bracelet, concho belt, or silver necklace. I hear her tell the children they can have them back when they go home for the summer, but she just tosses them in a box, so how will each child know which bracelet is his?

The youngest children begin to cry when the woman takes their jewelry. The unsmiling women then herd the children into the wide door at the top of the wooden stairs. The children's shuffling moccasin-covered feet stir up so much dust, it looks like they are walking in a thin layer of fog.

After a few minutes, another yellow school bus filled with silent brown faces screeches to a halt. I watch the boarding school's front door for any sign of the children who'd just entered; I'm worried about the crying Navajo children. I watch bus after bus arrive at the boarding school, and each time, the older children translate for the younger ones, the woman takes their jewelry, and then the kids disappear into the boarding school.

Just as I'm about to climb down from the garbage can tower, the door at the back of the boarding school opens, and brown-faced children flood the playground. I stand up tall on the tower and shade my eyes with my hands to see these children. They don't look like the same kids who arrived earlier.

Oh, my god! These children have been scalped! The boys have marine-style buzz cuts like Dad's, and the girls have short bob cuts like mine. The boys now wear starched, white, short-sleeved cotton shirts tucked into freshly pressed black wool slacks. The girls traded in their beautiful colorful blouses for starched white cotton shirts tucked into flared black wool skirts.

The youngest children don't seem to know what to do or where to go; they act like they've never see a tetherball or a big metal slide. Older boys and girls walk them around the playground; I imagine they are explaining its special features, such as the fastest speed of the merry-go-round or how to get on and off of the teeter-totter without smashing their fingers.

Within minutes the boarding school's playground fills with games of "Red Rover, Red Rover," tetherball, and hopscotch. After a while, an earsplitting recess bell fills the air, and the older Navajo children quickly push and shove the younger ones into a straight and silent line. One by one, the white starched shirts fade into the rear of the dark building.

The abandoned merry-go-round winds to a stop, and the tetherball slowly bounces off the metal pole. Dust devils speed around the playground and erase the children's footprints. One thousand Navajo children are my new neighbors, but I'm not supposed to talk to them.

The evening before my first day of school, Grandma spends the night with us because Mom is in Cortez with Marilynn. She curls my hair by spitting on small strands of hair, wrapping them around her middle finger, and then sticking two bobby pins in each curl. It takes a long time, and before I go to bed she wraps toilet paper around and around my head to help keep the curls in place. Then she kisses me on my nose. During the night Joellen stays far away from me so she won't disturb my curls. I'm anxious to see how my new curly hair will look. I want to look my best for my first day of school.

Grandma smiles at me in the morning as we hurriedly remove the toilet paper and bobby pins. We are both stunned at the result; one side of my hair is curled, the other straight. Dad pokes his head in my bedroom door, smiles, and says, "Perfect!" D'Nelle and Deanne take a look at me and laugh.

It's not perfect, and it's not funny. I hate Dad and D'Nelle and Deanne. Joellen takes the new barrette from her hair and clips it into my straight hair. The barrette slides down my thin, straight hair and hits the floor. Tears pool in my eyes. Nobody at school will like me. Grandma runs to the kitchen for a glass of water and quickly smoothes the curly side of my head with cold water. Now I have half a wet straight head and half a dry straight head. Perfect!

For my first day of school, I don't have a beautiful velveteen skirt or a red satin blouse, like the Navajo women at the trading post. I don't own any jewelry. My elementary school doesn't have big dark doors like the boarding school; it doesn't even have a slide on its playground.

As I stand in the hallway outside my new classroom, I think of Marilynn lying in her hospital bed in Cortez. She wants Joellen and me to tell her everything that happens on our first day of school. I wonder if I have to tell her about my hair.

Joellen nudges me in the back and says, "Don't be a chicken. Go on in. I'll see you on the playground at recess, and you can tell me everything you did, and I'll tell you what I did. Stop biting your lip, stand up straight, and have a fun time."

I stand in the doorway of my classroom, tugging on my upper lip with my bottom teeth, trying to hide my ugly twisted front tooth. I try not to think of how Marilynn would tease me: "You're too tall, and nobody reads Sherlock Holmes in the first grade." I concentrate on keeping my ankles straight so that I won't cave in the sides of my hand-me-down tennis shoes when I walk. A little white girl comes to stand beside me. She has wild, unrestrained bouncing red curls and a smile that seems painted on her face—it looks just like the smile on Joellen's Janet Lennon paper doll. I've seen this girl playing by the mobile home behind the trading post. Dad says her father is another holy roller. I follow her into the classroom and sit behind her.

Miss Mills, my teacher, has curly brown hair, and her stockings have thick straight seams that run up the back of her legs. A freshly washed green chalkboard dominates one end of her classroom. Stuffed into an empty soda pop bottle at the center of Miss Mills' desk is bright red crimson sage; its spicy scent permeates the room. Letters of the alphabet line the windows. Green-backed hummingbirds float in midair outside the window, as if they'd like to join us. Stacks of books titled *Dick and Jane at Work and Play* line the edges of Miss Mills' desk. I hope I don't have to read *Dick and Jane at Work and Play*. I might have to bring my own books to school.

Most of the children in my classroom are Navajo, and they look just like the Navajo children from the boarding school—short hair, starched white shirts, black slacks or skirts. My pink plaid shorts and striped shirt are out of place in this classroom full of black and white. The white kids who live in my compound and the Kerr-McGee compound and the white kids who live in Shiprock attend my school, but the majority of the kids in my classroom are Navajo. I don't know why some Navajo kids come to my school and others have to live at the boarding school all year. Mom says it's because the boarding-school kids don't live close enough to go home every day, so they have to sleep at the boarding school.

I glance from Miss Mills to the hummingbirds to the stack of books on her desk to the face of each child who walks into the classroom. The Navajo children creep silently into the room and slide into the nearest vacant seat. They keep their eyes directed at the floor. Miss Mills greets each arriving child with *ya'at'eeh* instead of hello. She says *ahehee'* instead of thank you. She walks from desk to desk, hugs each child, and then whispers something in their ears that makes them look up at her and smile.

I nervously bite on my upper lip in order to keep my new classmates and Miss Mills from seeing my twisted front tooth. Miss Mills leans down and hugs me. She whispers in my ear, "I love your pink shorts." I look up at her and smile. She turns to face the class, smiles to the classroom full of anxious brown and white faces, and says, *"Ya'at'eeh.* Welcome to first grade."

At lunchtime, Bonnie, the girl with all the curls, and I sit together at a cafeteria table. The first- through third-grade classes share the lunchroom, and the noise from so many voices makes it hard to talk to the person sitting next to you. The Navajo children who sit near Bonnie and me eat their food so fast you'd think they'd choke. The runny Jell-O and spaghetti without meatballs doesn't look that good to me. Bonnie smiles at the Navajo girl sitting beside her and says, *"hello."*

I poke Bonnie in the ribs. "Shut the fuck up," I tell her. "The Navajo kids can't understand English."

Miss Mills gently touches me on the shoulder and asks me to come with her. In an isolated corner of the noisy lunchroom, she explains that "fuck," "goddamn it," and "shit" are all words that she's heard from me this morning, but these are not words that I should be using. I tell her that my father, grandfather, and Marilynn use those words all the time. She is not persuaded by my argument. She changes her suggestion to a rule just for me: no "fucks," no "goddamns," and no "shits." I return to my seat next to Bonnie and conjure up all kinds of hateful things to do to Marilynn for not telling me that I shouldn't say those words in school.

Bonnie says nobody curses in her house; her dad is a minister. She lives in a mobile home behind the trading post and has two sisters and two brothers. All of the kids in Bonnie's family have names that start with B. After school, Bonnie walks with me as far as my house and then crosses the cattle guard and walks down the highway to her mobile home.

For two months, Mom and Dad drive back and forth to Cortez, and then, finally, they bring Marilynn home. For her homecoming, Grandma and Grand-dad help us blow up balloons and tape them around the house. Joellen and I make drawings and tape them on the wall by Marilynn's bed. Marilynn has missed so much while she was in the hospital that we want to make her part of the room extra special. When they arrive, Marilynn looks like she is really happy to be home, but she's much skinnier than when she left, and Dad has to help her walk to her room. When D'Nelle sees Dad helping Marilynn walk from the car, she runs to her room and cries. Lady barks and jumps in the air because she is so happy to see Marilynn.

Mom is still worried about her, and so she makes Marilynn come straight home from school each day and take a rest before supper. Although Marilynn looked a little pale when she arrived home from the hospital, she perks up right away when she gets to school. For Christmas, Mom and Dad buy her an expensive wooden clarinet and let her join the school band as a way of making up to her for letting her get sick and almost dying. My Christmas gifts are moccasins and a silver concho belt; I wear them to school every day.

Marilynn rapidly recovers, but whenever she doesn't want to do the dishes or sweep the floor, she pretends to not feel good. That's how she got out of helping Dad in March with his track-and-field practice. Joellen and I were sent to be Dad's guinea pigs instead of Marilynn.

Danalee and D'Nelle on float—Shiprock Fair 1958

Joellen and I approach the track behind the junior high school with caution; we're not sure what Dad wants us to do. He told us to show up at the track after school today. Tall, skinny, seventh-grade Navajo boys stand beside the carefully laid out track. Until recently, Shiprock didn't have a junior high school, and now that they do, they have new equipment for every sport, even bowling. They even have a trampoline in the new gymnasium. There are new team uniforms for each sport and new referee uniforms. Dad's new school has it all.

Dad spent days raking the dirt for the new track and laying down white chalk to define the race lanes. Dad sees us approach and waves his arm in frustration. "Hurry up and get to the fucking starting line. What took you so long? My boys have been waiting for fifteen minutes. We've got a track meet in five weeks, and these idiots aren't anywhere near ready."

Dad follows us to the starting line and continues yelling instructions. "Bend from the waist like you're waiting for the starter's gun to go off, and when I yell go, run down the track as fast as you can. I don't care which one of you wins."

He points to the group of Navajo boys standing beside the track. "These idiots keep crossing the finish line together. I'd like them to see one of you win the race."

Joellen and I tighten the laces on our old tennis shoes. We stand shoulder to shoulder at the freshly laid chalk line on the school's new track. From the finishing line, Dad yells, "Go!"

We speed down the lanes as fast as we can run. Joellen crosses the finish line first, and Dad makes a big deal of it to the group of Navajo boys. "She won. She crossed the line first. Get it?"

Dad makes us race over and over until we're short of breath and our heartbeats echo in our ears. I'm a much faster runner than Joellen, but sometimes I slow down and let her win. She wins. I win. She wins. I win. We never tie. When we are completely out of breath, we lie in the dirt on the edge of the field and clutch our throbbing sides.

The thin Navajo boys in their new gym uniforms approach the starting line. They are relaxed and smiling. They stand shoulder to shoulder, knees bent, elbows cocked, just like Dad shows them. They run down the track when he lowers his outstretched arm and yells, "Go!" As the speeding boys approach the finish line, the group slows and always manages to cross the finish line together. They laugh and congratulate each other on their joint victory.

Dad stands with his hands on his hips and shouts to his novice track team, "No! Goddamn it! Get back to the starting line, and do it again. This time, one of you try to beat the others, just like Joellen beat Danalee. One of you runs across the fucking finish line first."

Joellen and I sit beside the track and smile at the Navajo boys and encourage them to win. I watch them race and wonder if the boys at the boarding school have a track team. I see the boarding school kids playing on the playground, but that is all. I don't know what happens inside their school. Bonnie told me that the kids at the boarding school have to make their beds and do laundry and help cook the meals, like a giant family. If it's a giant family, it's sure a lot quieter than my family. The only noise from the boarding school is the monthly Navajo Chapter meeting. A bunch of Navajo men meet in the shade of the cottonwood trees each month and smoke cigarettes and talk about the things that Shiprock needs, or they give approval to people who want to build houses or businesses. Sometimes I can hear them talk if I sit on the garbage can tower but mostly, I'd like to know what goes on inside the boarding school.

Dad continues to drill his track team as Joellen and I head home. Spring days tumble into summer days. The Navajo boys on Dad's track team finally figure out that they are supposed to try to cross the finish line first. Once they figure it out, Dad has a pretty good track team. The last day of school rapidly approaches, and Bonnie and I plan on spending every day together during summer vacation.

By the time school is almost out for the summer, Mom is no longer concerned about my crossing the cattle guard and walking along the highway to Bonnie's mobile home or to the trading post by myself. I walk pretty much wherever I want to go in Shiprock. Joellen made friends with a boy who Granddad says is a half-breed. The boy—Shawn—was in her class at school, and she walked to his house after school on some days. Marilynn explains to me why Granddad calls Shawn a half-breed—Shawn's mom is Indian and his dad is white—but I don't understand what is bad about that. Marilynn is friends with Shawn's older sister—she has a record player at her house and orders records through the mail. Marilynn is looking forward to spending a lot of the summer listening to music. Joellen, Marilynn, and I decide to not tell Granddad that we have friends who are half-breeds; it's none of his business.

Four days before school is officially over, Joellen snuggles next to me in our bed in the early morning hours. We hear Marilynn humming a new tune and D'Nelle telling Deanne to stay in her own bed and leave her alone. We hear something else, too; we hear angry voices coming from the kitchen.

I put a pillow over my head to block out the voices, but I can still hear them. From her tone of voice, I can tell that Mom is furious with Dad. "What the hell do you mean, we should move this summer? I'm not moving again. I finally feel settled in this place. We've moved five times in the past seven years. I'm staying in Shiprock this summer!"

I take the pillow off of my head. Dad speaks in a slow, quiet voice, as if he's talking to one of his students. "I've told you, Jo, that if I take a couple of classes at the college in Las Vegas, I can get my teaching credential for New Mexico and make a higher salary."

"I'm not moving my children to Las Vegas!" Mom is still mad. "There are gamblers and killings and … and … prostitutes. How can you even consider such a thing?"

Las Vegas sounds like an awful place. I'm with Mom; I don't want to move there.

Dad continues in his soft tone. "I told you; it's Las Vegas, New Mexico, not Las Vegas, Nevada! It's about a three-hour drive from here. We can lock up this house for the summer and rent a furnished place in Las Vegas. All we'd need to do is take some clothes for the few weeks we'll be there. Once I get my teaching certificate I can teach anywhere in New Mexico. We can get off the reservation if you want to. Jo, we really need the money; you know we do."

The fight in Mom's voice melts. "I don't want to move again. We just got this place fixed up. It's not fair for you to even ask this of me."

I hate the idea of moving to Las Vegas. I whisper to Joellen, "I'm not going. I can live with Grandma, and the rest of you can go."

Joellen retorts, "I'm not going, either. I can live in the hideout under the boarding school's playground. Brother Frank can bring me food."

Marilynn, who's stopped humming and has heard everything, chimes in. "Idiots. Brother Frank won't bring you food, and there's no room in Grandma's little mobile home for anyone but her and Granddad. We're all going to fucking Las Vegas because Mom's a fucking mush brain. She should stand up to Dad and tell him to go by himself."

From across the hallway, D'Nelle announces, "I'm gonna tell Mom you said 'fucking.' I want to go to Las Vegas."

Deanne never knows what she's saying. She sings over and over again, "Fucking Vegas! Fucking Vegas!"

Marilynn mumbles to herself, "God, please make them go away." She shouts across the hall to D'Nelle and Deanne, "Oh, shut up!"

I wish Dad would go to Las Vegas by himself. Who's going to stay with Grandma when Granddad's delivering gasoline, if we live three hours away?

PART II

Navajo Taboo: Do not try to count the stars or you will have too many children.

○ ○

Alaska and Hawaii become states.

The Navajo Times, *the reservation's first newspaper, publishes its first issue.*

3

Las Vegas, New Mexico, 1959

The sound of Lady's panting fills the car during our three-hour drive to Las Vegas. Someone at the college found a house for us, and Dad starts school tomorrow. It's funny that an old person can go to school. Mom sits silently beside Dad; she is back to not being excited about too much. She's unhappy that we left Shiprock. Before we left, she taught Vicky how to play bridge, and they played two-handed bridge every day. Now she wants to teach Marilynn how to play bridge, but Marilynn isn't interested.

Dad stops the car in front of our rental home, and Mom's gasp vibrates through the car. It looks like it might fall over if the wind blows too hard. Marilynn hates it. Mom hates it. D'Nelle refuses to go inside, just in case it does fall over.

It is a sad-looking house, with shingles missing from the roof and paint peeling from the siding. The porch sags to one side. The inside of the house looks better than the outside; it has three bedrooms so that Marilynn, Joellen, and I can still stay away from our two little sisters. Deanne doesn't care where she sleeps, as long as Lady can sleep with her.

Mom cries for the first few days but then settles in and tries to clean the kitchen and make macaroni and cheese for us. I guess Las Vegas might not be too horrible, but I miss Grandma and Granddad and Bonnie. On our fourth day in town, a sheriff's car parks in front of the house, and a sheriff talks to Mom and Dad for a few minutes. I wonder who's in trouble or if Lady has done something wrong, but then I really get scared when the sheriff makes Dad and Mom follow him back to his station.

Marilynn takes advantage of Mom and Dad's unexpected disappearance by suggesting that we move all of the furniture in the living room into a big circle and make a giant fort. We work together, pushing the couch and chairs together. We get the clean sheets from the hall closet and hang them over the furniture. Deanne and D'Nelle climb under the sheets and giggle.

Dad walks through the door about the time I'm ready to climb under the sheets. "Jesus H. Christ! What the fuck are you doing? Marilynn, go and pack a suitcase with some of your mother's things. Joellen and Danalee, you two get some clothes together for you and your sisters. We need to drive to Farmington right now, and then we'll drive back to Shiprock and spend the night there."

A stunned Marilynn asks, "Why? What's happened?"

Dad turns his back on her. He grabs a bottle of beer from the refrigerator and goes in the bathroom and slams the door. Marilynn and Joellen and I silently start gathering clothes. I peek out the front door. Mom sits on the front seat of the car, crying—but it's more than crying. Her whole body trembles. Her head leans against the car's window, and tears run down the glass. She is lost in a world of sadness that I have never seen before. Fear crawls into my belly, and vomit rests in my throat. I continue packing clothes.

The three-hour ride to Grandma and Granddad's mobile home feels endless. Finally, we arrive at the Royal Trailer Court in Farmington. Granddad's Texaco Star tanker truck partially blocks the roadway. A state patrol car is parked in my grandparents' gravel driveway. Its circling red and blue light reflects off the dusty metal side of my grandparents' single-wide mobile home.

Grandma and Granddad's mobile home park is not really like a park, with slides and swings; there is just a bunch of really old mobile homes. It's the only place that Granddad could find for them to live when they rushed to Shiprock when Marilynn got sick. Dad pulls in next to the patrol car. Even though it's late, it is still hot. With all of the car's windows rolled down, Lady still pants like she needs a drink of water, and Deanne and D'Nelle sweat while they sleep on the backseat of the car. Their short blond bangs stick to their foreheads, and moisture gathers at the back of their knees.

Mom and Dad walk to the front door of Grandma's house, but the state trooper who stands by the front door won't let them pass by him. In the silence of the late evening, I can hear everything—the crickets chirping, the bugs buzzing around the porch light, and the state trooper's words: "We're waiting for the coroner to arrive and take the body. Everyone is next door."

Mom and Dad walk next door. Like a broken record, my mind is stuck on his words, "take the body." Whose body? Granddad is fifty-six, so I guess he's old enough to die. Grandma is only forty-six, so she can't die. "Take the body" rumbles through my head, and the taste of vomit returns. I think I will die if something has happened to Grandma.

While we wait, the patrol car's circling light fills the darkness of our car. I've never known anyone who has died. I don't know anything about God, but I pray and pray that Grandma isn't the one who is dead. I know it's mean to want Granddad to be the one, but Grandma is my best friend. She's taken care of me since I was born. She just can't be dead.

D'Nelle and Deanne sleep soundly. Lady stops pacing inside the car and lies down beside Deanne and sleeps. Marilynn sits on the backseat; she hugs her knees to her chest and rests her head on top of her knees. I know she is not asleep, but she doesn't want to talk. Joellen rests her head on the rim of the open window and stares into the darkness. I fix my gaze on the front door of the neighbor's house and say in my mind, over and over again, "Please let Grandma be alive."

Mom and Dad finally emerge from the neighbor's mobile home. My heart collapses when I see Granddad walking with them toward the car. Mom and Dad each hold one of Granddad's elbows, and they gently guide him down the wooden steps and toward the front passenger side of our car. Granddad walks like he's wearing lead-lined cowboy boots. Dad's compact athletic body seems much taller and stronger tonight. Mom trembles and takes giant gulps of cool night air. She needs just as much support as Granddad.

It's a good thing I don't go to church because at this moment in time, I hate God. I hate Granddad for being the one who's alive. I hate Grandma for doing this to me. I feel like my internal organs are exploding all at once, and the resulting particles are sucked into a bottomless crevasse that I cannot see or touch. In my mind, I try to cling to the sides of this invisible crevasse, to grab onto something—anything—to prevent Grandma from falling away from me.

My mind silently screams, "Wait, Grandma! Wait! Don't go!" I begin to slide down the sides of the crevasse, spiraling around and around toward nothingness. Nothing can prevent me from dying right along with Grandma.

"A city in England," she says.

"What?"

I feel like I am in a dream. In my dream it is one week earlier. I am sitting on the worn couch in my grandmother's mobile home, the day before we leave for Las Vegas. I'm holding a cup of cold coffee, Grandma's special concoction—one-third coffee, one-third sugar, and one-third milk. The aroma of our breakfast of fried eggs, bacon, and toast mingles with the smell of tobacco. My chalk-like candy cigarette with the pink tip is balanced between my lips. *Sherlock Holmes* lies open on the couch beside me. With my left hand I absentmindedly pick at the dried red clay lodged under my big toenail. Granddad is away for a few days delivering gasoline, and it is my turn to stay with Grandma.

She says, "*Fifteen down. A city in England. It's six letters.*" She sits at the little fold-down table in their tiny dining room. The Formica surface is peeling around its edges. The table is just big enough to hold her dog-eared crossword puzzle book, a fresh pack of Lucky Strikes, her morning cup of black coffee, and some letters she recently received from her friends and family in Texas. Last month she complained to me that with the cost of first-class stamps going up to four cents, she wouldn't be able to afford to write letters to her friends in Texas.

I ignore the opened letters, terrified that one day she will decide she is sick of the blowing dirt, the heat, the typhoid scares, and the Indians, and she'll move back to Texas. Life would end without Grandma.

Her right leg is curled under her left, and with her left hand she picks at the dry, cracked skin on the heel of her right foot. Her slightly pudgy body barely fits into the narrow bench-type seat. Except for a few crow's feet and dry heels, at the age of forty-six, her naturally tanned skin is smooth. Her shoulder-length brown hair is tied up under a fine net, like the one the cook at the local diner wears, but a few gray strands poke through the top of the net. A silver chain grips the ear-pieces of her pointy-rimmed glasses.

An ever-present smoldering cigarette balances between her lips. It bounces up and down when she talks, but the ash never falls onto her crossword puzzle book or into her coffee. Thick smoke slithers upward, causing her to squint, but she never moves the cigarette. The pencil twiddles back and forth between her index finger and middle finger as she contemplates the clue.

"*London,*" I tell her. Sherlock Holmes is good for something.

"*London, of course. What a little smart-ass.*" Grandma always thinks I am smart.

Mom, Dad, and Granddad all sit in the front seat of the car. Before we leave, Mom's teary eyes meet mine. She doesn't have to tell me; I know Grandma is dead. Dad starts the car and we drive for thirty minutes to reach our house in Shiprock. We spend one night there and then drive to El Paso, Texas, where Grandma is to be buried. I don't understand why Grandma is being buried in El Paso. She was born in Uvalde, just like I was and Mom was and Grandma's mom was. Just because Grandma's mom, Mammy, and her sister Sallie live in El Paso, I think that's a dumb reason to bury Grandma there. All of her friends are in Uvalde.

Granddad's family has a great big family plot in Uvalde's cemetery, right next to the man who used to be the vice president of the United States. Granddad told me all about it, and he also said that he's supposed to be buried there and

Grandma is supposed to be buried next to him. Mom and Dad have everything all messed up.

Mom and Dad don't care what I think. Dad just wants to get the funeral over with so that he can go back to school in Las Vegas. Granddad doesn't seem to care what happens. He's barely alive, now that Grandma is dead. Mom hasn't slept in two days. She's back to being a zombie. Marilynn's acting like the boss and telling my sisters and me what to do.

It's a very long drive from Shiprock to El Paso, and we are the last to arrive at Mammy's tiny house in El Paso. Mammy is unhappy that we have a dog with us, but she lets Lady stay in her backyard while Mom and Dad go to the funeral. Mammy is tiny, like her house, and she dresses in black from head to toe. Grandma isn't the first of Mammy's children to die; her son Wade died when he was just twenty-three. Grandma has a picture of Wade on her dresser at home.

Grandma's younger sister Sallie is there—she's tall and thin, just the opposite of Grandma. Mom's older sister Betty and her husband, Bob, and their three kids are eating the turkey sandwiches that Mammy made for them. Betty is a little crazy. I mean, sometimes she's happy, and she plays her guitar and sings when we visit, and then sometimes she hates to see us and just wants us to go home. We never know which Aunt Betty will meet us at the door. Today, she hugs Mom the minute she sees her, and the two of them sit in the corner and cry. Mom's little brother isn't here because he's in the Marines and stationed in the Philippines.

Mammy isn't used to having so many people in her house. I sit in the living room next to Granddad and try to ignore everyone. My eyes are glued to Granddad's face, and I'm mad at Mom because she's not going to let me go to the funeral. How can I be too young to say good-bye to Grandma? Mom and Aunt Betty are making all of us kids stay home, and that makes Marilynn as mad as hell; she thinks she's old enough to go to a funeral.

All of a sudden, Mammy stops what she's doing and announces to the crowd, "It was God's will."

Like a bunch of robots, the rest of the adults agree. Betty dabs her tears with a tissue and offers, "She now has eternal rest."

Her well-meaning husband, with his mouth full of turkey sandwich, agrees. "The angel of death has taken one of his finest."

Granddad's gaze is rooted to the floor. Snot dangles from his upper lip. He says nothing. I scoot over next to him and hold his lifeless hand and wipe his nose with my tissue. Dad stares at sad-eyed Mom and whispers, "Honey, she's gone but not forgotten."

Mom's silence does not hold back the hatred that simmers in her return gaze.

I stare at the adults and think, *Doris, the cadaver, has expired … departed … passed on … been laid to rest … unfortunately caught by the jaws of death … and was most certainly gone. She will never, however, be forgotten.*

The adults go off to the funeral, and my cousins, sisters, and I stay at Mammy's and eat the turkey sandwiches, potato chips, pickles, and cookies, and we drink all of her milk. Stuffing ourselves with food doesn't make any of us feel better. When the adults return, Dad is anxious to drive back to Las Vegas and return to school. Mom is anxious to make sure Granddad is all right before we leave. He is supposed to go home with Aunt Betty and stay with her for a while.

Dad sits on the arm of the chair where Mom is sitting and pleads with her. "Jo Eva, it was a cerebral hemorrhage. There was nothing you or anyone else could have done that would have saved her. Come on, now—I need to get back to school. Skeet can stay with your sister for a few days. Then he can get back to work. His neighbor promised to have the blood cleaned up from the bedroom before your father returns. He'll be all right."

Mom stares at Dad; she's as shocked as I am. "He can't 'get back to work.' He thinks he's having a heart attack."

Dad is losing patience with Mom and with all of us. "And the fucking doctor said earlier today that he isn't. Doris has taken care of him all of his life; he's just going to have to adjust to life without her."

Mom hasn't budged from her chair, "You're a cold-hearted son of a bitch. We can stay here for a few days until he feels better."

Dad hasn't budged from his desire to leave. "No, we can't. Right now, taking care of my own goddamn family comes first, and I need to finish these two classes and get my teaching certificate. Get yourself and the kids ready; we're driving back to Las Vegas … now."

Dad wins. Mom hugs Mammy, Betty, and Sallie and stomps off to the car. Marilynn, the boss, herds the rest of us into the car. Before I leave I hug Granddad and whisper in his ear, "It'll be all right. I'm still your little shit."

Skeet and Doris wedding day

4

Michael

I spend a horrible summer in Las Vegas. Dad receives his teaching credential and a raise in salary. Mom spends most of her time talking on the telephone to Aunt Betty to see how Granddad is doing. I think Granddad hasn't done well because the day we return to Shiprock from Las Vegas, Uncle Bob arrives with Granddad and leaves him with us.

Granddad takes over the bedroom where Marilynn, Joellen, and I have been sleeping, and we now sleep on the living room floor. Granddad doesn't talk to anyone; he hardly ever leaves the bedroom. Mom tries to get him to join us for supper, but I haven't seen him eat anything for three days. Dad runs off every day to the junior high school and says he has to get ready for classes. I think he just doesn't want to hear Granddad crying or Mom pleading with Granddad to eat something. All of the neighbors stop by to tell Mom how sorry they are that her mom died. Vicky makes supper for us on the days when Mom just stays in her room, like Granddad, refusing to come out.

The wooden floor in the living room is cool, and the room is quiet and a good place for sleeping, except for the sound of crying. Marilynn flops around on her makeshift bed. "I hear him," she announces. She gives up on trying to sleep and leans back against the couch. She repeats herself, as if I didn't hear her the first time, only this time she says it louder. "*I hear him.*"

I close my eyes and try to sleep, but I can't sleep and watch for cockroaches that also live in my house, at the same time. School starts in a few weeks, and I'm not going to be able to walk if I have to keep sleeping on our living room floor. Mom doesn't have the heart to tell Granddad to go home. I think Marilynn just needs to learn how to ignore Granddad and go to sleep.

Marilynn leans over and jabs at me with her foot. "He's crying again."

I don't know what she expects me to do about it. "So?"

Marilynn doesn't know when to shut up. "He's getting snot all over your pillow."

I give up on sleeping. Joellen is sleeping and doesn't care if Marilynn and I talk to each other. I turn to face her. "So? It's my pillow, not yours."

"Go make him stop. Go on. Make him stop." Marilynn must think I have magical powers. "Tell him to go home. I'm tired of sleeping on the floor. I want my own room back. He likes you. Go tell him." Marilynn is desperate to sleep in her own bed. "Please, Danalee, you're the only one he listens to. Tell him to go home."

I hate to be the one to break it to Marilynn, but I heard Mom and Dad talking yesterday, and I think Granddad is here to stay. I debate whether I should tell Marilynn the bad news; maybe she'll figure it out for herself. On the other hand, if I tell her Granddad's not leaving, maybe she'll stop bugging me and go to sleep. "I think he *is* home. I heard Mom tell Dad that Granddad was going to live with us from now on."

Marilynn forgets to whisper and yells at the top of her lungs. "*What?* What about my room? I want my room back!"

From down the hall Dad yells, "Shut the fuck up and go to sleep!"

In the few remaining days before school starts, Dad remodels our duplex once again. Our bedroom becomes Granddad's bedroom, and the old wall that once separated the duplex living rooms goes up and my sisters and I now have our own bedroom again, right next to Granddad's. Mom and Dad drive to Farmington and bring back a new bed for Granddad—he says he can't sleep in the same bed he shared with Grandma. Mom drives his 1953 white Buick to Shiprock and parks it next to the duplex. She puts all of Grandma's dishes in our kitchen cabinets and all of her clothes in Mom's closet. The picture of Wade goes on Mom's dresser.

In an odd way, having Grandma's dishes and clothes and the picture of Grandma's baby brother around makes me feel less lonely; it feels a little bit like having her live with me. Now if Mom and Granddad would only stop crying, I'd feel a lot better.

The only place in Shiprock that makes me feel happy these days is the secret hiding place by the river. The cool bark of the fallen cottonwood tree never changes. The birds, butterflies, and humming birds are always happy to see me. Squirrels, chipmunks, horned toads, and mice live in the hollow parts of the tree.

As I lie on my back on top of the fallen tree, tears sneak up on me, and I can do little to stop them. I feel lost without Grandma. Since her death I've felt as if a giant adult hand is holding my head under the muddy waters of the San Juan River. I can see the light through the surface of the cold, dark water, and if I had any energy I might reach the surface again and begin to breathe, but I have no energy for living.

If I knew where she went after she died, I'd run away and join her. Marilynn told me that Grandma is in a wooden box in the ground in El Paso, and by now the bugs are eating her brains. When she said that I covered my ears and screamed, "Shut the fuck up!" I wish Marilynn didn't know everything.

Sometimes when I climb up onto the fallen tree, I lie on my back and just stare at the clouds. Bonnie told me that the Navajo believe that staring at the clouds will make a person a slow runner, but I don't care. I can see Grandma in the clouds, smiling down at me, and then the wind comes and blows her away. In my head, I write letters to Grandma and send them off to heaven. In today's letter I write:

Dear Grandma,

Grandma? Grandma can you see me from heaven? Are the bugs eating your brains? I miss you, and Granddad misses you. What are we going to do without you? Please help Mom learn how to cook. Please help Mom stop being mad at Dad. Please don't let the bugs eat your brains.

Joellen sneaks up on me as I lie on the tree and tells me that Dad is wondering where I am; we head home. Joellen and I are supposed to keep an eye on D'Nelle and Deanne while Marilynn cooks supper. Marilynn knows how to cook one thing—Sloppy Joes—and she's pretty good at it. D'Nelle and Deanne are easy to look after since Granddad's come to live with us. They won't come out of their room for fear of meeting him in the hallway. Granddad has become very scary. He cries all day and all night. Tears flow nonstop from his swollen eyes; his breath shudders on the intake. The caved-in, shriveled cheeks of his toothless mouth look like they are collapsing in on themselves. He hasn't shaved since Grandma died, and as far as I can see, he hasn't eaten anything, either.

When we are at home, Marilynn, Joellen, and I keep our bedroom door closed, day and night, to keep out the thick blue smoke of his self-rolled cigarettes. When he's not in his bedroom crying, he sits outside under the cottonwood tree next to the duplex and stares into space. An endless supply of tears and snot stream down his unshaven face. Granddad hasn't gotten any better since Grandma died. One evening after supper, D'Nelle announces, "Granddad stinks. Mom, Granddad needs a bath."

"He'll take a bath when he's ready," Mom explains. "Go play in your room, and you won't have to smell him."

D'Nelle is not persuaded. "But I can smell him from my room. His room is right across from my room. Let's throw him in the bathtub, clothes and all. That would make him laugh. Come on, Mom, let's do it. That would make Granddad laugh."

Marilynn looks up from her homework. "He's catatonic. Nothing will make him laugh."

Mom doesn't feel like laughing, either. "Off to bed, everyone. Granddad will get better when he's ready. You'll just have to ignore him until then."

Late that night, Marilynn and Joellen and I lie in the dark and listen to muffled crying.

Marilynn complains, "He's crying again."

I say, "No, he isn't."

Marilynn knows what she hears. "Is too. I hear him."

I can tell the difference between Granddad's crying and Mom's crying. In our new bedroom we are much closer to the kitchen, and we can hear everything someone says—there's no door to the kitchen. I whisper to Marilynn, "It's not Granddad; it's Mom."

Marilynn sits up in her bed. "What's wrong with Mom?"

"If you'd shut up," I point out, "we could hear Dad talking to her."

Marilynn, Joellen, and I sit in our beds, arms wrapped around our bent legs, and concentrate on the voices coming from down the hall.

Dad speaks softly. "Honey, I don't think this is the right time to go through with this. Let's wait a few months, when things have settled down."

Mom's voice isn't soft, it's determined. "I'm not waiting. I told Mr. Yazzie we'd take Michael when we came home from Las Vegas. It isn't his fault that Doris died. We've put it off long enough."

I hear her set her bottle of Coca-Cola on the kitchen table. Mom is always stronger when she's drinking a Coke. Grandma used to tease Mom that she'd die without a Coke.

Dad sounds like he is trying not to make Mom cry. "I know we said we'd adopt Michael, but your father is not going to like this. He didn't like the idea when we talked to him and Doris about it, and he isn't going to like it now. Putting a baby in his room is not a good idea."

Mom is not crying now, and she is not giving in. "Well, Joe, what do you expect Michael to do? Keep living with a family that doesn't really want him? It's not his fault that his mother died. You and I and Mom all thought this was a good idea. The only thing that has changed is that Mom isn't here to help, but I can do this. You still want to adopt him, don't you? I still want to adopt him. We'll make room for him somehow. He needs us. I'm driving over tomorrow to meet Michael and bring him home for a visit, just like we planned. He's only fourteen months old. Doris wouldn't want me to abandon this poor child."

Joellen makes sure the voices have stopped before whispering in my ear, "Who's Michael, and why's he coming home with Mom?"

I try to remember if Mom or Grandma said anything to me about a Michael. I don't think they did. I whisper back to Joellen, "I don't know. Marilynn, do you know who Michael is?"

Marilynn, already lying down in her bed and trying to sleep, offers a brisk reply. "Nope, but I'm not giving up my room again."

I lie in bed and think about what Mom said. I don't understand—why are we adopting someone named Michael? Who is he? How come Grandma knew about this and didn't tell me? How come Granddad thinks it's a bad idea? I don't think Granddad is going to notice anything, not even one more kid around here. Where is Michael going to sleep, and who's going to change his diapers if Grandma's not here to do it? Can a fourteen-month-old even walk?

The next day my sisters and I hang out in the shade on the porch of the old schoolhouse. We all want to see Michael when Mom gets home with him. Four-year-old Deanne thinks having a baby brother is a great idea. She wants him to sleep in her bed. D'Nelle is more reserved, unsure of what it might mean to have a brother. I'm nervous and angry. Mom and Grandma and Dad should have told me about this; I don't like surprises. Granddad wanders out to his rocking chair that's under the cottonwood tree and now, like the rest of us, he's going to see Michael when Mom gets home with him.

The red station wagon rattles across the cattle guard, and Mom parks the car next to the duplex. A chubby Navajo boy stands on the seat beside Mom with his arm wrapped around her neck. She doesn't get out of the car right away but just stares through the front window at her welcoming party. The little boy smiles at us, and deep dimples pierce his smooth brown skin. He is very pudgy and has creamy brown eyes. I understand now why Granddad is not going to like Michael—my new brother is an Indian. Mom gets out of the car and reaches back inside for Michael. He clings to her and is afraid to get down. I can hardly blame him; we must look as strange to him as he does to us.

D'Nelle stares at Michael and asks Mom, "Is Michael an Indian?"

Mom pulls Michael closer to her. "Yes, he is. Michael's mother died a few months ago when she was giving birth to Michael's half brother. Michael's

Navajo uncle, Mr. Yazzie, can take care of Kevin, Michael's baby brother, but not Michael. Before she died, Grandma and your Dad and I all agreed to let Michael live with us. He's your new baby brother. Michael will stay with us every day for a few weeks, until he gets to know us, and then the Navajo court will sign a paper, and Michael will officially be your brother. He's a little scared, so I'll just hold him for a while."

Mom walks into the house to find Dad. It's amazing to have four sisters one minute and four sisters and a brother the next. I wonder if Michael will like us. I wonder if he will miss his baby brother. I wonder why his aunt and uncle can't take care of him, but they can take care of his baby brother. I wonder where Michael is going to sleep—I hope it's not in my room. I hear Dad's happy voice greeting Michael: "There's my little guy."

Michael, 1960

After a few minutes, Mom and Michael come outside and approach Grand-dad. Michael, now toddling along beside Mom, holds tightly to her hand. He really is cute; I like him instantly. Mom bends down so that Granddad can see her face without having to look up and speaks in such a quiet voice that, from the porch, I cannot hear what she says. Granddad doesn't usually hear what you say anyway. He still spends most of his day staring into space and crying. It looks like he heard what Mom said, though, because he stands up from his rocking chair so fast that the chair flips over backwards. Michael starts crying so hard that Mom picks him up. I can hear what they are saying now because they are yelling at each other.

And Granddad says the first words any of us have heard him say since Grandma died: "You've brought a goddamn injun into our house! Have you lost your fucking mind? Get that filthy thing away from me!"

Michael hides his face in Mom's shoulder. She stands her ground and tells Granddad, "He's going to live in this house, and he's even going to share your bedroom. Doris thought this was a fine idea, and so do I. You have a new grand-son—get used to it. If you don't like it, you know where the door is." Wow! Mom's not even drinking a Coca-Cola, and she's acting braver than Marilynn.

Granddad doesn't like Indians or Mexicans, and he's not going to like having Michael around.

During his first visit Michael stays for three hours, and then Mom drives him back to his uncle's house. Mom says that Michael's uncle lives in one of the new wood-framed houses near the hospital that is being built. It's a tiny house, and that's probably why he doesn't have room for both Kevin and Michael. We live in a small house, but we have room for Michael by letting him sleep in Grand-dad's room. Granddad is so mad at Mom that he packs his 1953 white Buick and drives to Las Cruces to stay with Aunt Betty.

He is gone for two weeks and during that time, Michael comes to the house every day. I think he is getting used to having five sisters, and we all like playing with him. He plays with our Lincoln Logs, and he really likes my Tiny Tears doll. When he first arrives each day, Michael sits in Mom's lap, and she talks to him in English so he can learn English words. She plays with him and reads to him. D'Nelle waits in the hallway for Mom to finish so that she can have a turn with Michael. Deanne entertains Michael by running around and around him, yelling, "Look at me! Look at me!"

Dad pinches Michael's cheek and smiles at him. Lady somehow seems to know that she is bigger than Michael; she cautiously approaches him and lets

Michael pull her long fur. I change his diapers and tickle him. It is great having a baby brother.

Granddad comes home at the end of two weeks and throws his clothes back into his room. While he was gone, Mom set up a crib and put in a little dresser for Michael's clothes. Granddad stares at the crib and dresser, but he doesn't throw them out. The first day that Granddad is home, he and Michael take a nap together in their room. Mom paces up and down outside of the room, just to make sure that Michael is all right.

We plan a little party for the day when the Navajo judge signs the paper that makes Michael our brother. Each time it's time for Mom to drive Michael back to his uncle's house, I can tell that Michael would rather stay with us. Once the paper is signed, Michael will live with us all the time. Today, two days before the signing party, Michael's stepfather, Johnny, is coming to pick up Michael, and then he will drive over and pick up Michael's half brother so that he can visit with them. Johnny is Kevin's dad but Michael's stepdad. None of us want Michael to go with Johnny, but Mom says that Johnny has the right to see Michael, so he's going.

Mom and I watch Johnny's beat-up truck bounce across the cattle guard. Mom holds Michael. She has a little lunch packed for him and some diapers and bottles. Johnny is a short, skinny Navajo with pock marks across his cheeks. Like most traditional Navajo, he doesn't look Mom in the eye when he talks to her. He says that he will return Michael later today, and he thanks her for the lunch and bottles. Michael cries the moment that Mom sets him on the front seat of the beat-up truck. We hear his cries until Johnny's truck is out of sight. Mom cries and runs into the house. I sit in the shade on the porch of the abandoned school-house and wait for Michael to return. I wait and I wait, but Michael doesn't return.

"Goddamn it. Son of a bitch. I should have known this would happen." Dad paces the floor in the living room, six hours after Michael was supposed to be home. Mom sits at the kitchen table with tears running down her face. My sisters and I also are crying. I'm in a state of shock; I feel a little like I did when Grandma died. Earlier, Dad drove over to Michael's uncle house to see if Michael was there, but Michael's uncle hadn't heard from Johnny.

Granddad sits across the kitchen table from Mom, eating his favorite snack, a sardine and mustard sandwich. He is not as upset as the rest of us. With his mouth full of sardines, he says, "Good riddance. Michael needs to live with his own kind."

Mom gets up from the kitchen table and moves to the living room. I think as long as Michael is around, Mom doesn't have to think about losing Grandma. Losing Grandma and losing Michael may make Mom permanently crazy. I don't want Mom to go crazy.

Dad's going crazy just waiting. He stops pacing up and down in the living room. "Jo, I'm going over to Mr. Yazzie's house to see if they've heard anything. I'll be back in a while. This would sure be a hell of a lot easier if the Yazzies had a telephone. Danalee and Joellen, why don't you two come with me? Marilynn, you can get D'Nelle and Deanne ready for bed. We shouldn't be too long."

Marilynn gives me her "I hate you" look as I leave the house with Dad. She's going crazy being trapped in the house with Granddad and Mom. When I'm outside, I hear Deanne begging, "Read to me. Marilynn, please read to me."

Joellen and I sit in the backseat of the car and don't talk. The dirt road to Mr. Yazzie's house is bumpy and dark. Construction equipment lines the sides of the road; Shiprock's new hospital is scheduled to open in the spring. I haven't paid too much attention to the new hospital because I won't be able to go to it; I'll have to drive to Cortez just because I'm white. I guess Michael will get to go to the new hospital if he ever gets sick.

Driving down the dark road to Mr. Yazzie's house, I fear something horrible has happened to Michael. When we reach Mr. Yazzie's house, Dad waits in the car, like a good Navajo visitor, until the front door opens and Mr. Yazzie acknowledges our presence. I'm glad Vicky has helped Mom and Dad learn how to be good Navajos.

Mr. and Mrs. Yazzie don't have any children; maybe that's why they wanted to keep Michael's half brother, Kevin, for themselves. When we are inside their small house, Joellen and I sit at the kitchen table. While Dad and Mr. Yazzie talk, Mrs. Yazzie offers us a piece of fry bread with honey on it. I lick the honey off my fry bread and watch Dad as he listens to Mr. Yazzie. I can't hear Mr. Yazzie's soft voice from where I'm sitting, but Dad looks like he doesn't like what he's hearing. He listens and then shakes his head from side to side. He and Mr. Yazzie finally say good-bye, and we climb back into the car and drive down the dark, bumpy road in silence.

After a few minutes, Dad stops the car and says, "Shit!"

My lower lip trembles. I struggle to keep from crying. I want to know what's happened to Michael, but I'm too afraid to ask Dad what Mr. Yazzie said. Joellen is curled up into a knot on the seat next to me. Her arms cover her head in an attempt to stifle the sounds of her crying.

Dad turns around and puts his arm on the back of the front seat. "Girls, Mr. Yazzie is afraid that Johnny has taken Michael and Kevin to live with him." Dad's voice sounds like he's been crying. "He doesn't know where they are but he has some friends trying to find them. He's going to let me know as soon as he finds Michael. But we have to be prepared for the possibility that they may not find him. When we get home you're going to have to be strong and help your mother. We're going to all miss Michael very much."

I pound the backseat with my fist and moan, "But he's my brother. How can Johnny just take him? He's not even Michael's real dad." I don't understand how Johnny can take Michael; the Navajo judge said he was my brother. Kevin is a tiny baby—how can Johnny take care of him? It's not fair! Granddad was getting used to having Michael sleep in his room, and now he gets a room all to himself again. It's not fair!

When Dad tells Mom the news, she doesn't think it is fair, either. Everyone in the house hears Mom wail, "No-o-o! No-o-o!" My sisters and I sit huddled on the bottom bunk bed in D'Nelle and Deanne's tiny bedroom and listen to Mom cry. Granddad is strangely silent. Marilynn tries to explain to D'Nelle and Deanne why Michael may not come to live with us.

Mom, Dad, my sisters, and I wait for word from Mr. Yazzie. The next day, Mom drives to Window Rock where the Navajo judge gives her one piece of paper that says she is Michael's legal mother and another piece of paper that says whoever has Michael has to give him back to Mom. After several weeks, Mr. Yazzie's friends find Johnny, Michael, and Kevin living in a motel room in Los Angeles. Mom is going to take her piece of paper from the Navajo court and ride the bus from Farmington to Los Angeles to find Michael and bring him home.

The day before her trip, Mom packs the old brown suitcase that Dad used to take on his golfing trips. She's never been to Los Angeles, so she isn't sure which clothes to pack. I beg to go with her, but she tries to convince me that it's better if I stay here. She packs and talks at the same time. "You and Joellen will have fun staying with Vicky and her family while I'm gone. Her two boys are just about your age, and you can all walk to school together. And Vicky's house is very close to Bonnie's house, so she can walk to school with you, too."

I sit on the edge of her bed and try to change her mind about making me stay with Vicky. If I can't go with her on the trip, I'd rather stay home than stay with Vicky. "But Mom, I'll be just fine right here. I can help Marilynn with Deanne and Granddad, and I can ..." I struggle to think of what I can do. "I can keep the house clean."

Mom closes the lid to the old brown suitcase. "Nope. You and Joellen are staying with Vicky. D'Nelle is staying with Shane's family. and Marilynn and Skeet can take care of Deanne and the house. Dad will be busy with the start of school, so it's better this way. I want you to do your homework and not give your Dad or Vicky any trouble. I should be home in nine or ten days."

I'm shocked! Nine or ten days! How can I start second grade without Mom here? Who's going to comb my hair and make my lunch? I like Vicky, but I don't want to live with her. I go back to my original strategy of getting Mom to take me with her on the trip. I hop off of the bed, lift Mom's brown suitcase to the floor, and casually say, "Why can't I come with you? I can keep you company. It's a long bus ride, and you'll need some company, and Michael will be happy to see me, too."

She ignores my suggestion. "Go tell your dad that I'm ready to leave. I left a map for you on the kitchen table. You can draw a line along the path that I'll take to Los Angeles. You can figure out where I am each day. It's a big bus, and I will have lots of company, so you can stay here and do what I ask you to do."

When Dad and Mom leave for the bus station in Farmington, I find Farmington on the New Mexico map that Mom left for me. With my finger, I follow the line from Farmington to Albuquerque, Mom's first stop.

Joellen and I walk to Vicky's house after Mom and Dad leave for the bus station in Farmington. Vicky's house is made out of big round rocks; it is cool inside, much cooler than our house. Vicky shows us where we will sleep until Mom comes home—on the floor in the bedroom with Vicky's two young sons. So far, this isn't fun like Mom said it would be. And now I can't find the bathroom. I've looked in every room in Vicky's house. Every house has a bathroom; where's Vicky's? Finally, I give up the search. Vicky is working in the kitchen, so I ask her, "Where's the bathroom? I need to go to the bathroom really bad."

Vicky points to the side door in the kitchen. "Our bathroom is outside, honey. It's that building next to the fence. Just lock the door so no one comes barging in on you."

The outhouse has a big wooden door. It's a big door because the outhouse is almost as big as our duplex. Large red clay tiles line the floor. A shiny new toilet sits to one side of the room, with a big white sink next to it. On the back wall, a white cast-iron claw-foot tub rests on the red clay tiles, like a king's crown. I flush the new toilet and run back to the house. I announce to Vicky in a breathless voice, "I need to take a bath before I go to bed. Mom said I needed to take a bath today. Can I do it now? Please?"

Joellen stares at me and corrects my line of reasoning. "No, you don't. It's not Wednesday. Our day for a bath is Wednesday. What's the matter with you?"

What's the matter with me? Joellen obviously hasn't seen the bathroom. I ignore Joellen and plead my case to Vicky. "Vicky, I got extra dirty today helping Mom pack. I know I'll feel better if I have a bath. I promise I won't use too much water. Please, Vicky? Please?"

Vicky gives me the go-ahead, and Joellen gives me the "are you insane?" stare.

Once I'm back in the outhouse, I lock the door and take off my clothes. I turn on the faucet and watch the hot water slosh from side to side in the big, deep tub. The water slides up and down the sides of the cast-iron tub and finally settles into the bottom. My foot turns bright pink when I step into the steaming water. I slide into the tub with the water still running. When the water reaches my waist, I turn it off and slide down into the tub until my ears fill with water.

Warm, salty tears slide down the sides of my face and join the bath water. I cry until I have no tears left, until my nose is so stuffed up that snot can't find its way out. I cry until the bath water turns cold and goose bumps begin to form on my thighs. I'm so afraid of losing someone else I love. I write Grandma another letter in my mind:

Dear Grandma,

Please! Please watch over Mom, and don't let anything bad happen to her. And please keep Michael safe until Mom finds him. Grandma, can you see me in this great big bathtub?

Each day Vicky looks at the map with me and helps me find the towns where Mom's bus will travel that day. Mom has traveled from Farmington to Albuquerque and she still has two more days on the bus before she reaches Los Angeles. In the evening Vicky tells us stories about the Navajo so that we can learn more about their beliefs. The one I like the best is story of how the Navajo became such great weavers. Someone named Spider Woman taught them how to weave on a loom made of sun rays and lightning bolts; I'd love to see that!

I learn from Vicky that Navajo kids who live at the boarding school have to help keep the school clean and the classrooms clean and their bedrooms clean, and they have to study and go to school. They don't get to see their moms or dads or brothers or sisters until they go home again in the summer. Vicky says lots of kids never return to the boarding school, once they are old enough to herd the sheep on their parents' land.

On the fourth day that Mom has been away, Dad stops by Vicky's house to tell us that Mom will be home in four days, and Michael will be with her. Dad wears his famous grin and his blue eyes twinkle when he tells us. I can go home in four days and sleep in my own bed and listen to Granddad complain. I'll miss the big bathtub at Vicky's, but I'm ready to go home, and I can't wait to see Michael. I wonder if he'll remember me.

Four days later I stand in the middle of the highway and watch for Dad's car; he's gone to Farmington to pick up Mom and Michael. My heart pounds so hard that I feel like my eardrums are going to burst. I jump up and down and spread my arms wide and twirl around and around when I see the car approach. When Michael gets out of the car, my sisters and I all try to hug him at the same time. We laugh and cry, and Michael seems a little afraid of us and holds onto Mom's hand and won't let go.

After supper he seems more like his old self and toddles to each one of us and receives another hug before settling down into Mom's lap. She's promised to tell us everything that happened on her trip as soon as Michael goes to bed, but he's only moved a few feet from her since they got home. He's not ready for bed, so she starts her story with Michael on her lap. I sit on the floor beside her chair in the living room and think to myself how lucky we are to have Michael back.

Mom shifts Michael's chubby little body from one leg to the other, trying to find a comfortable place for Michael to rest on her lap. She finally gives up trying and starts sharing her story. Mom speaks softly so that Granddad can't hear her. "On the first bus, I sat right behind the driver, and no one sat next to me. On the second day—"

Joellen raises her hand as if she's in school and interrupts Mom right away. "Wait. Wait. Who else was on the bus? How many people?"

Mom hugs Michael and smiles at Joellen. "Now, let's see … there were some Navajo men sitting in the back of the bus, and a couple of white women with their children sat across the aisle from me. A really old man with white hair sat two rows behind me, and he snored really loud when he fell asleep." Mom makes a big loud snoring sound, and we all laugh.

From the kitchen, Granddad yells, "Keep it down out there!"

Mom raises her eyebrows at Granddad's interruption and then continues in a quiet voice, "When we stopped in Gallup, everyone got off the bus and had some supper. I sat on a bench in the lobby of the bus station and ate my peanut butter and jelly sandwich and one of the popcorn balls you made for me. They were just delicious. I saved the other popcorn ball for Michael. When I finished eating I watched the sun set. The sky turned red and orange, and it looked like a giant fiery ball had fallen off the edge of the earth. Everyone climbed back onto the bus, and a few more people joined us. By the time the bus reached Phoenix, everyone on the bus, except me, was sleeping."

D'Nelle interrupts this time. "Mom, everyone on the bus except you and the *driver*. The driver wasn't sleeping." D'Nelle is reading all of my Sherlock Homes books, and she prides herself on her ability to solve mysteries. She looks at me and smiles; she knows that I appreciate her ability to solve mysteries. Marilynn thinks D'Nelle is turning into a bookworm, just like me.

Mom also appreciates D'Nelle's logic, and she leans down and touches her cheek. "You're right, sweetie, not the driver. He stayed awake the entire time. We got a new driver in Phoenix, and the old driver and the old loud snorer got off the bus. Anybody who wanted to get off the bus and run to the bathroom could do so, and when everyone was back on, the new driver left Phoenix and headed for Los Angeles.

"It was late at night and very dark when we left Phoenix. I took a little nap, and when I woke up the sun was shining, and the bus was stopped in a small town. Most of the people from the bus were having breakfast inside the bus station. I felt a little silly, sleeping through the stop. I ran to the bathroom and then walked around the bus five times to get the kinks out of my legs."

Before Mom can continue Deanne, who was almost asleep, sits up straight and suddenly decides to pay attention. "Kinks? Mom what are kinks? Did they hurt?"

Mom smiles and reassures her, "Kinks means that my muscles were all tired from sitting on the bus for a day and a half, and walking around helped me stretch my muscles and made them feel better."

Deanne returns to leaning against Marilynn's back and is almost asleep again; she didn't really care about the answer to her question. Michael is also almost asleep, but Mom shifts his weight to another leg and continues with her story.

"The new driver tipped his hat to everyone on the bus and then headed out to the highway. I stared out the window and thought about each one of you. I wondered what you were doing and if you were okay. I missed you very much. We stopped in lots of little towns, and it took a very long time to reach Los Angeles, a whole day. Early on the morning of my fourth day on the bus, we pulled into the bus station in Los Angeles. The bus station was bigger than your school, and hundreds of people were hurrying to catch a bus."

Marilynn knows that Hollywood is in Los Angeles. She reads the *Teen* magazine that comes on the bookmobile every month. She's careful not to wake Deanne as she asks Mom, "Did you see any movie stars? There are lots of movie stars in Los Angeles."

Mom tries not to hurt Marilynn's feelings. "Well, hon, I think the movie stars were probably still sleeping when I arrived. It was very early. But Johnny's sister and her three little girls were waiting for me."

Mom finally gets to a part of the story that interests Dad. He doesn't care about being quiet. "What was she like?" he asks.

Mom thinks for a minute and then answers. "Well, she's probably younger than I am, maybe twenty-seven or twenty-eight, and she was very nice. She dressed like a white woman and drove an old beat-up Chevy. Her kids were eight, six, and four and very quiet. Sally talked nonstop about how ashamed she was of her brother's behavior. She didn't know Michael's mother, Margaret. Johnny married her when Michael was only two months old, and then Margaret got pregnant right away with Kevin. Sally, like Mr. Yazzie, has no idea who Michael's father is or if he's even alive. Sally didn't know that Michael's mother had died until Johnny showed up in Los Angeles with Michael and Kevin. She said that Johnny has been using the boys to collect Margaret's Social Security death benefits. He needs the boys to prove that he is the surviving parent and that he's taking care of them. He gets about $150 a month from the Social Security office."

Dad can't believe it. "He's using the boys to run a scam? What a son of a bitch!"

Mom acts like she would just like to forget the whole thing. "I'm happy to be home. I don't want to take another bus ride for a long, long time."

Dad still has a few questions. "Well what happened when you and Sally reached Johnny's motel?"

Joellen is interested in this part. She sits up on her knees and says, "Yeah, did you pound on the door and then punch Johnny in the nose?" She is all excited, thinking about Mom punching Johnny in the nose.

Mom raises her eyes at Joellen's comment and tells us, "When we got to the motel, Sally went to the door first, and I stayed in the car with her girls. She talked to Johnny for a few minutes and then signaled for me to come inside. I walked past Johnny without speaking to him, and when Michael saw me, he ran over and wrapped his arms around my legs so tight that I almost fell over.

"Kevin was sleeping on the floor, and Sally picked him up and took him with her. I picked up Michael and we left. I didn't say one word to Johnny, and I didn't have to show him the paper from the judge saying Michael was legally mine. Sally and I just left him standing in the doorway, and she drove us back to the bus station, and I bought two tickets for home. Kevin will stay with Sally until Mr. Yazzie arrives to get him. When the bus arrived, the driver said I had to sit in the back with the Indians, so Michael and I sat on the very last row of seats, and he fell fast asleep."

I'm surprised that Mom and Michael had to sit on the last seat, but Marilynn doesn't seem to be. She reaches out and touches the Band-Aids® on Michael's legs. "What happened to his legs? Why does he have Band-Aids®?"

Mom pulls Michael closer to her and whispers so that she won't wake him up. "We'll have to leave the Band-aids® on for a while. It looks like Johnny burned Michael's legs in several places with a cigarette. I have some medicine on the burns, but I want you all to be careful and not touch the Band-Aids when you change his diapers."

Joellen reaches over and touches Michael's arm. "I hate Johnny." Tears pool in the bottom of her eyes. "Let's never let Michael out of our sight again."

Mom wipes tears from her own eyes and smiles at us. "What did you do while I was gone?"

D'Nelle decides not to fall asleep on the floor. She sits up and announces, "Danalee danced on a float."

Mom stares wide-eyed at me. "You did? When did you do this?"

I'm proud that I get to be the first one to tell Mom what I did while she was gone. "It was for the Navajo Fair. There was a parade on the first day of the rodeo, and each class decorated a float, and then some kids got to ride on it. Bonnie and I and a bunch of other kids rode on the float that my class made. Then we went to the rodeo and watched the bull riders."

Joellen loved the bull riders. "Yeah, I want to be a bull rider."

Marilynn's eyes get all dreamy as she tells Mom, "They let me watch the *Kinaaldá* dancers. When I'm thirteen, I'll be old enough to dance in the ceremony. Mom, did you know that after they dance in this ceremony the girls are eligible to be married? The Navajo girls looked beautiful. This year the Fair was really something, Mom. Navajo families came from all over the reservation, almost ten thousand people, and just camped in their wagons and pickups. Next year, when you're with us, we can buy jewelry and moccasins and rugs much cheaper than at the trading post."

Mom smiles at a sleepy D'Nelle. "And what did you do at the Fair, little lady?"

D'Nelle didn't like the bull riders, and she didn't get to ride on a float, and she isn't thirteen years old so she couldn't dance with the Navajo girls. She thinks for a minute and then reports, "I ate seven pieces of fry bread with honey, and then I got honey on Granddad's pants, and then he told me to fuck off, and then Dad—"

"All right. All right." Mom gets the picture. Her legs look numb from Michael's weight. She lifts Michael up to Dad, who carries him off to bed. "I'm very happy to be home, and now you all need to get to bed and get some sleep. You have school tomorrow."

The burns on Michael's legs heal by the time Halloween arrives, but he is too young to go trick-or-treating with us. D'Nelle wants to be the Navajo person called Spider Woman for Halloween, but I talk her into being my assistant, Dr. Watson. Granddad makes a Sherlock Holmes-type pipe for me out of wood, and Mom helps me make a hat.

Deanne is a ghost. She has an old sheet with holes cut out for her eyes, nose, and mouth. Mom ties a rope around her waist so she won't trip on the sheet. Marilynn and Joellen leave early to trick-or-treat with their friends. I think Marilynn is too old to trick-or-treat; she should stay home and hand out the treats, and then Joellen would have to go with us.

When my sisters and I start trick-or-treating, the schoolteachers compound is dark. Tiny yellow porch lights and a near-full moon help guide us from house to house. Miss Mills, D'Nelle's teacher, lives in the first house past our old mobile home. The lights are off at her house; she drives into Farmington for Halloween and never hands out treats.

Mrs. Whitman, my second grade teacher, and her husband are just the opposite. Each Halloween they pace back and forth on the wooden boards of their tiny front porch, watching for trick-or-treaters; they love them. Mrs. Whitman makes fudge with walnuts in it for a treat. Some kids go to her house twice.

My sisters and I trick-or-treat our way around the schoolteachers compound. Our brown grocery bags grow heavy. We make several stops to eat something out of our bags to help make them lighter. As we approach the last house in the compound, we see an old lady with white hair standing on the porch, waiting for us. Mrs. Thomas, Joellen's third grade teacher, studies us through her thick, metal-framed glasses. A white apron covers her gingham dress. Thick tan hose cover her skinny legs. Mr. and Mrs. Thomas live in the house next to the stile that leads across the fence to the Kerr-McGee compound. (I can see her husband inside the house, asleep in a rocking chair.) When we leave their house, we'll climb the stile and trick-or-treat in the Kerr-McGee housing compound.

Mrs. Thomas stands on the edge of the porch and stares down at us. "Dana-lee? Is that you? My, you have a scary little ghost with you."

Deanne giggles and says, "Boo."

I hold my cardboard magnifying glass higher and wiggle the wooden pipe in my mouth. "I'm Sherlock Holmes," I inform Mrs. Thomas, "and this is my assistant, Dr. Watson." D'Nelle straightens her back and wraps her cape closer to her body.

Mrs. Thomas claps her hands. "Wonderful, just wonderful! You're the best I've see all night."

Last year I discovered that Mrs. Thomas always tells everybody that they are the best she's seen all night. We add the candy to our bags, but before Deanne, D'Nelle and I can climb onto the first step of the stile, Laura, a second grader who lives in the Kerr-McGee housing compound, runs up to us, shouting in a panicked voice, "Danalee! Danalee! There's a monster at your house! When it growled we all dropped our popcorn balls and ran as fast as we could. I think it might be Rock Monster. He's really, really tall and has a hairy monkey face. He's growling like a lion. Your mom is screaming at him, trying to make him go away!"

I drop my bag of candy and grab Laura by the shoulders. "Stop! Stop!" I yell at her. "Is my mom all right?"

Laura calms down a little. "I don't know. She's yelling ... she's yelling words I'm not allowed to say. But she yanked the monkey's face right off, just right off!"

Deanne starts to cry. I try to think like Sherlock Holmes. I don't think a giant hairy monkey is attacking Mom. I look Laura in the eyes. "It's okay. I won't tell anyone what you say. Tell me what my mom yelled when she yanked the monkey's face off."

Laura leans closer to me and whispers so Mrs. Thomas will not hear her, "You goddamn fucking idiot; this is not funny."

That's what I thought! I reassure Laura and Deanne and D'Nelle that Mom is okay. I promise to give Laura a new popcorn ball tomorrow. She is too afraid to continue trick-or-treating by herself, so I tell her to trick-of-treat with us. D'Nelle wants to know how I know that Mom is okay and that a big hairy monkey-faced monster is not eating her, right this very moment. I stare at D'Nelle and finally tell her that the monkey-faced monster is Granddad wearing his old raccoon coat that we've seen a million times. I don't know where he got a monkey mask.

D'Nelle is impressed and bows before me. "Sherlock Holmes solves the mystery of the monkey mask."

While D'Nelle is bowing, Deanne runs up the stile and heads off to trick-or-treat in the Kerr-McGee housing compound. I follow her across the stile and wonder when Granddad is going to stop acting so crazy.

5

Daniel

The cool porch of the old abandoned schoolhouse is a good place to be on a hot May afternoon. It feels hotter this year than last, but I've discovered that Shiprock's weather is either boiling hot or freezing cold, with not much in between. I escape to the porch when I need a quiet place to read. Michael's second birthday is approaching, and Deanne and D'Nelle are in their room, arguing about who gets to color the birthday card.

I place my book aside and watch as a pregnant Navajo woman, with a stomach so big it looks like she might need to deliver her baby right now, paces in front of the duplex's door. I know she's waiting for Mom to see her and ask her to come in. Dragonflies circle the woman's large, round belly. She's beautiful. A long purple velveteen skirt shimmers in the late afternoon sun. A fine layer of dust covers her moccasins and the edge of her skirt. Her tongue nervously licks dry, chapped lips. Wisps of black hair escape the bun at the base of her neck and float against her neck. Silver and turquoise bracelets hug her left wrist.

I wonder if she's some unseen neighbor who's stopped by to complain about Marilynn's nonstop practice on her clarinet. Marilynn practices every day. The slender black case of her precious instrument rests beside her pillow each night. She's threatened to cut off our fingers if Joellen or I touch it.

When Mom finally appears at the doorway, she smiles and says "Ya'at'eeh" to the Navajo woman. With that greeting, the Navajo woman begins to talk fast. She nods her head and points with her lips toward Michael, who is playing in the yard. The Navajo consider it rude to point with their fingers; they gesture toward what they are talking about with their lips. I leave my book on the porch and move closer to Mom.

The Navajo woman refuses to come inside and sit down, but she accepts the glass of water that Mom offers. Mom and I don't understand what the woman wants or why she won't come inside and cool off and have something to eat and drink. The Navajo woman seems focused on Michael, but we can't understand why. Mom decides that we should drive the woman to the trading post to see if Jim, Vicky's husband, can help us, but the woman won't get in the car. When she hears Jim's and Vicky's names, though, she finally gets into the car. Mom hollers at Marilynn to take care of the kids until we get back. As we bump over the cattle guard and head down the highway, I see Marilynn standing at the door of the duplex, wondering what is going on. Like Vicky, Jim's been in Shiprock a long time, and the Navajo trust him. He knows most of the tribal members who live in and around Shiprock, and he speaks Navajo. We hope he'll know this woman and will be able to explain to us what she wants.

After speaking with the woman, Jim tells Mom that the woman's name is Mary. She is approximately eight months pregnant, and she wants Mom to take her sixth child, an eleven-month-old boy named Herman, and make him well, like the fat Navajo baby she saw playing in our yard. If Mom makes Herman well and Mary delivers a baby boy, Mom then can have the new baby boy, and Mary will take Herman back. But if Mary delivers a baby girl, then, she says, Mom can keep Herman, and Mary will keep the baby girl.

We already have learned that in the Navajo world, women are more important than men—they own the hogan and the herd of sheep. Jim says that Mary is afraid that Herman may die in the hogan, and if that happens, she will have to take her other five children and move someplace else. If someone dies in a hogan, the family is supposed to move out, but with five other children, that would be pretty hard for Mary to do.

Jim says Mary wants Mom to drive out right now and take Herman out of the hogan. Jim isn't sure where Mary's husband is, but he does know that Mary's husband is a drunk and can be abusive. He warns Mom to be careful if she encounters Mary's husband at the hogan.

Mom is amazing. She doesn't say that she needs to think about it. She doesn't say that she needs to go home and talk to Dad. Instead, she thanks Jim for his help. Then she helps Mary into the front seat of the car, tells me to get in the back, and off we go. All Mom says is, "What a wonderful birthday present for Michael—a new baby brother."

It is a strange ride out to Mary's hogan. Red dust swirls around the rear of the car as we drive slowly down the isolated dirt road that leads to the hogan. Sitting on the front passenger seat, Mary stares straight ahead, sipping the cool glass of water that Jim insisted she take with her. I watch the backs of the two women sitting in front of me, both mothers of six. One of them is going to give away her youngest child today. I wonder if Mom ever wants to give one of us away. Sometimes I wouldn't mind if Marilynn went away again.

I've never been inside a hogan but I know that lots of Navajo live in this kind of home. It's a six-sided mud-and-stick building, with a doorway that faces east—it faces east to bring the Navajo good luck. There is a hole in the center of the roof for the smoke from the fire ring to escape. I can't imagine living in a hogan with Granddad and Michael and my sisters. I think I'd go crazy.

Mary's hogan has a wooden sheep pen beside it, and a collection of tumbleweeds has gathered against the pen. There is an outhouse, but this one isn't nearly as nice as the one at Vicky's. The door to the outhouse hangs from one hinge, and a swarm of black horseflies circles the top of an uncovered latrine.

Mom parks the car near the door to the hogan. Five children stare at us from the doorway. The oldest child looks like he's about Marilynn's age; I think I've seen him at school. I don't recognize any of the other children. Mary walks slowly into the hogan; Mom follows her. I hurry out of the car and stay close to Mom. The kids follow us into the windowless space, partially blocking what little light and fresh air the open doorway provides.

The intermittent buzzing of green-backed flies ricochets off the cool mud walls. Herman's brothers and sisters hang back in the shadows. The dark eyes of the oldest child never leave my face. I wonder if he's angry with me. His expression is hard to see in the shadows, but it feels as if he holds me personally responsible for what is about to happen.

Even though there are nine people in the small mud-walled house, the absolute silence of everyone in the room heightens the feeling of solitude. Mary must have told her children about her plan to give Herman to a white family; they appear resigned to the fact that their baby brother will be taken away.

The cradleboard that holds Herman is laying on the smooth dirt floor on the other side of the fire ring. As I approach, I see flies hovering above Herman's face, and the odor of sickness grows strong. He does not look at me or smile. He looks like he is barely breathing. His stomach stretches out in front of him, like an overinflated balloon. His motionless legs and arms look like tiny twigs, ready to snap. Scaly, ringworm-covered brown skin hangs from his bones. Large black eyes stare straight ahead under half-closed lids that are caked with dried green mucus. A slimy yellow substance is crusted around his nostrils, making it hard for him to breathe. Persistent flies buzz around the slow trickle of brownish yellow pus that oozes from his left ear.

Mary unties the leather straps of the cradleboard and gently removes Herman. She slowly hands him to Mom. Their eyes focus only on Herman. The expressionless siblings silently watch as Mom carries Herman from his home.

I follow Mom into the late afternoon light and climb into the passenger side of our car. I wonder if Herman's brothers and sisters believe that this is Herman's chance to live, that giving him to a white family is better than watching him die. Maybe they believe Herman will return to them one day, healthy and strong, or perhaps Mary is simply protecting herself and her other children from having to leave the hogan, should Herman die. Giving your baby away to save your house seems heartless to me.

When I'm situated on the front seat, Mom places Herman in my lap. Yellow mucus drips from his ear onto my pink cotton blouse. Head lice dance on the top of my right hand. My shorts grow wet from his urine-soaked cloth diaper. With my hands trapped under his head and bottom, I can't shoo away the pesky flies that hover around his ears.

I hold my breath so that I don't have to smell him, and I close my eyes so that I don't have to look at the sad faces of his brothers and sisters. I hope Herman doesn't die on the way to his new home. Mom watches the dirt road but also continually glances at Herman. I think she is also afraid that he might die on the way home.

When we bump across the cattle guard, Herman tries to open his yellow-crusted eyes. Mom parks the car and turns to smile at me. She says in a cherry voice, "Well, I guess I'd better go in and tell Dad about Herman. Wait here until I get back."

Herman and I sit in the front seat of the car while Mom explains Herman to Dad. I don't need to be in the house to hear Dad's reaction. I hear him say, "Are you fucking crazy? We can't feed the ones we have."

Mom's voice sounds calm and comforting. "Now, Joe, just come outside and take a look at him. He needs us. I'm going to give him a bath, and then we can drive him over to the hospital and let them take a look at him. The new hospital has lots of room and a bunch of new doctors and nurses. Someone there will know how to help him. It's hard to believe he's almost a year old. He can't even sit up by himself."

I haven't moved—I can't, until Mom lifts Herman off of my lap. My sisters and brother stare through the car window at Herman and me. D'Nelle pokes her head in long enough to announce, "He stinks."

Mom reaches in and gathers up Herman in a clean blanket. "I know he does," she says. "Why don't you run in and start some bath water for him? I'll need to drive into Farmington tomorrow and buy some clothes for him."

Joellen stands at the front of the car, far away from the activity. "What's his name?"

I climb from the car and stare at my soaking-wet shorts from Herman's stinky diaper. "It's Herman," I tell her. "He has a bunch of brothers and sisters. He lives in a hogan. Marilynn, I think his oldest brother is in your class."

Mom interrupts my flood of information. "Thank you very much, Miss Know-It-All. Go in and change your clothes, and I'll tell everyone about Daniel."

I stare at her. "Who's Daniel? Jim told us that his name is Herman."

"That's his Navajo name," Mom announces. "I thought we'd name him Daniel, Dad's middle name. Now, you run on in the house and change those clothes. Then you can come with me when I talk to Skeet."

The last thing I want to do is be with Mom when she talks to Granddad. I know he's heard every word that's been said since we got home. You can hear anything that anyone says in this house, unless the person is whispering. Granddad is probably sitting in his room, smoking a cigarette, and just waiting to see where Mom thinks she's going to put this baby.

I feel better in my clean, dry shorts and blouse until I hear the volcanic eruption that takes place in Granddad's room. He isn't interested, he says, in having another goddamn injun in his room; Michael is bad enough. He wonders if Mom has lost what little mind she has. He reminds her that she and Dad can barely feed the bunch of kids they have. Does she think that she is some fucking Florence Nightingale? Does she think that her expert knowledge of babies is going to keep this kid alive?

Mom just lets the volcano erupt. When Granddad stops yelling and starts rolling another cigarette, Mom asks me to help her move Michael's crib closer to Granddad's bed so that she can place a crib for Daniel in the room beside Michael's. For tonight, Daniel will sleep in an empty dresser drawer in Mom and Dad's room. Mom hopes to get a little bit of milk into Daniel before she goes to bed. Daniel whimpers most of the night; no one really gets any sleep.

The next morning, Mom and Dad drive Daniel to Shiprock's new hospital. Dad plans to drive two hundred miles tomorrow to the Navajo tribal council in Window Rock, where he can pick up the adoption forms—we will either adopt Daniel, if Mary has a baby girl, or Mary's new baby boy, if she wants to take Daniel back. I wonder if Mom will name the new baby Daniel if we don't get to keep this Daniel.

Daniel has to stay in the hospital for a long time. He has to learn how to swallow food and not throw it up. The doctors take some skin from his leg and build an eardrum for him in his left ear. Once they do that, the yellow ooze stops dripping out of his ear. His right eardrum is damaged, but they can't do anything about it. They put some special medicine on his ringworm to make it go away, but the ringworm scars won't go away. Mom visits the hospital every day, and when the doctors are finished with him, Daniel comes home to live with us. While he was in the hospital, Mary gave birth to a baby girl, which means we get to keep Daniel.

Shortly after Daniel comes home from the hospital, my sisters and I started calling him "Danny"—he doesn't seem like a serious Daniel—and we start calling Michael "Mike," just because it's shorter. Danny learns to sit up, crawl, and smile. Like Mike, he doesn't seem to mind Granddad's cigarette smoke or grumpy ways. For Mike's second birthday, he's received the best present of all—a baby brother.

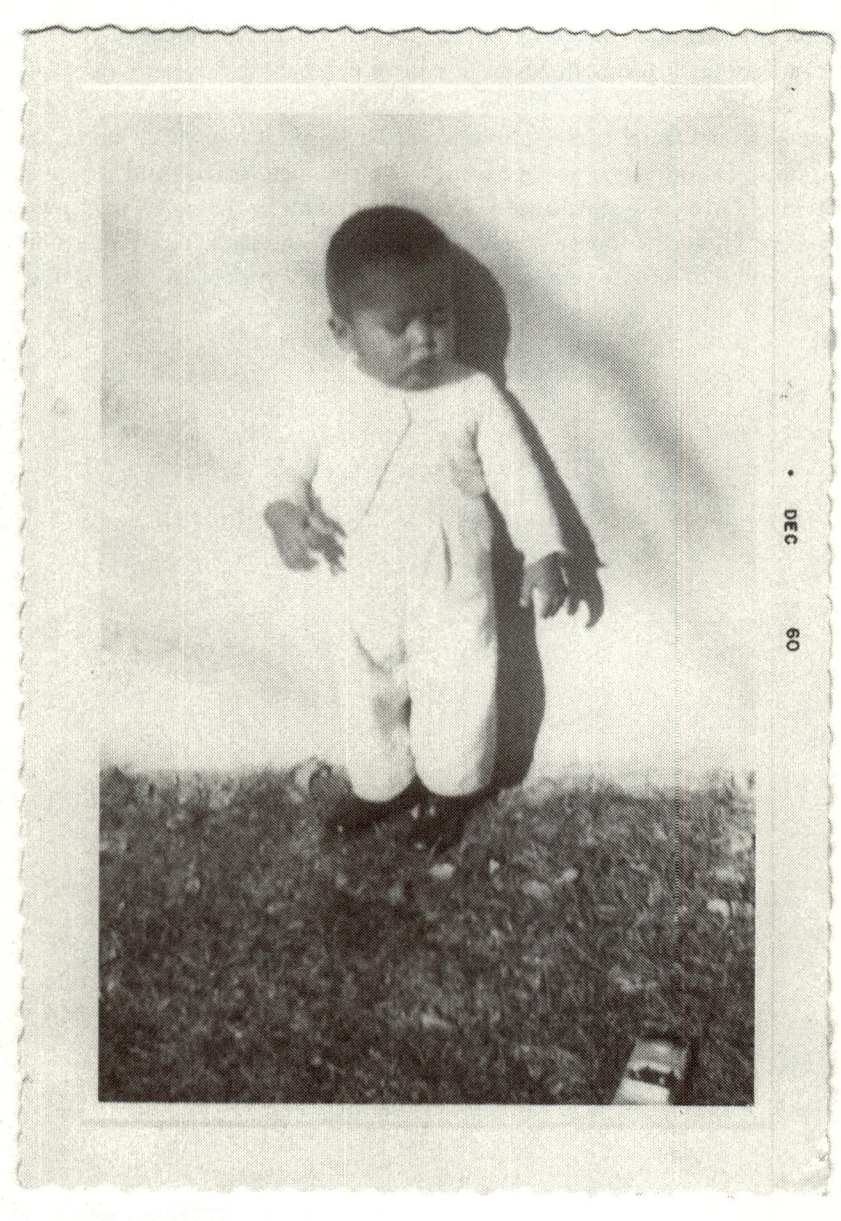

Danny—1960

6

Mom and Me

Last Christmas, Mom and Dad promised me that I could have my crooked front tooth straightened this summer while school is out. Today, Mom and I drive to Cortez to visit a dentist who will put braces on my crooked tooth and give Mom some new teeth. Mom and I visited the dentist last month, and he said I could have braces and that Mom needed some new teeth. He told her to stop drinking Coca-Cola, but that is like telling Mom to stop breathing.

My trip to the dentist starts off great—it's just Mom and me in the car, driving to Cortez. No Marilynn teasing me about my crooked tooth. No D'Nelle sneaking into my special box of books that I keep hidden under my bed. No Deanne talking and talking and talking about nothing. The only people I miss are Joellen, Mike, and Danny.

When we reach Dr. Love's office, Mom waits in the tiny waiting room while I have braces put on my teeth. It really, really hurts. When I'm finished, it's my turn to wait in the waiting room for Mom. I have to wait for a long time, much longer than Mom had to wait for me. My lips start to become un-numb; they tingle and burn, both at the same time. I still can't feel them, so every time I try to drink water, I dribble it down the front of my blouse.

Dr. Love's receptionist and I both jump when we hear a small scream from Dr. Love's office. I look to the skinny receptionist, hoping she will tell me what's happening, but she just gives me a faint smile and asks if I need to go to the bathroom. She's an idiot; of course I don't need to go to the bathroom. I need to know what's happening to my Mom and if that was her scream. Before I can ask her what has happened, we both hear Dr. Love's soothing voice: "Jo, I know it hurts. I'm sorry. But we are almost finished. You need to lean over the basin and spit. Come on now, spit."

It sounds like Mom's new teeth hurt more than my braces. I take the skinny receptionist up on her offer to go to the bathroom and then settle in for a long wait.

Late in the afternoon, the door to Dr. Love's examining room opens. He's holding the left elbow of a woman who, to my surprise, is dressed like Mom, but this woman looks like she's been in a car accident. Her hair lies matted to her temples, and perspiration stains the underarms of her white cotton blouse. There is bloody cotton-like stuff sticking out of her mouth, and her face is so swollen that it is hard to tell who she is.

Dr. Love guides the bloody-mouthed woman to one of the reception room's plastic chairs and helps her sit down. He then turns to me. "Danalee, here are the instructions for your mother to follow before the two of you come back next week. It is very important that she not remove the pink plastic mold that is covering her gums. Do you understand? Danalee? Pay attention. Do you understand? Now, help her to the car. You two have a long drive back to Shiprock."

I just stand there and stare at Dr. Love. I stare at the nervous receptionist. I stare at the drooling woman, who now stands next to me and searches for my hand.

Dr. Love and the receptionist stand in the open doorway and wait for us to leave. We have been the only patients he's seen today. The woman who is dressed like my mother takes my hand. The pain of my own braces has dulled my senses. The woman who is dressed like my mother *is* my mother! With Mom's full weight leaning on my left shoulder, I gather all of my strength and help her walk to the car. She slowly lowers herself onto the driver's seat and gently leans the side of her head against the car window. Her eyes close and blood drips from the sides of the pink foam that is stuffed in her mouth.

I run around to the passenger side of the car, crawl in beside her, and promptly wipe her teary face with the tissues that Dr. Love gave me as we left. With the first touch of my hand, she pulls back from me, jerks open the car door, leans her head out, and vomits. Saliva and bits of breakfast ooze past the intruding pink foam and drip onto the hot, cracked asphalt of Dr. Love's tidy parking lot.

I roll down all of the car's windows, and for a long while we just sit in the car and cry. Eventually, she starts the car, grasps the steering wheel, and guides us out of town to the old highway that runs the forty miles between Cortez and Shiprock. Once there, she pulls to the side of the road and vomits again.

As I watch her sides heave and see her face grow more swollen every time she leans down to throw up, I realize that we might not make it home. When she stops vomiting, she sits in her seat, sinking farther and farther down. She leans forward and rests her forehead on the backs of her hands as they grip the top of the steering wheel. Blood and spit from her toothless gums drip onto the floor of Dad's spotlessly clean car.

Eventually, she slowly lifts her head and tries to smile at me. She motions for me to get as close to her as possible and then reaches over and grabs my hands. She places them on the top of the steering wheel. I scoot as close to her as I can get without touching her face or neck, and she starts the car. She maneuvers us slowly onto the deserted highway. I lean across her trembling body and try to steer the car. Eventually, I sit in Mom's lap and push the pedals and steer the car. Mom is only half awake.

I drive very slowly. I keep swallowing my tears and snot and try not to drip onto Mom's lap. I squint my eyes to keep track of the fading white center line.

Mom groans when the car bounces over the cattle guard. I start braking long before I reach the car's parking spot beside the duplex. I don't want to run it into the side of the house. I can hear Dad as he walks out to greet us: "What the fuck?"

I park the car beside the duplex and turn off the ignition. Mom hasn't moved in hours. I don't know if she is alive or dead. Marilynn and Joellen stare into the car. Marilynn is mad and then confused. "Did you get to drive?" she asks.

Dad opens the driver's door and gently unpeels my fingers from the steering wheel. He whispers in my ear, "Come on, hon, let go. You're home now. Go on in and get to bed." But I can't go in and get to bed; Mom is still bloody and looks like she's dead.

Dad carefully removes me from the car and then leans back in to get Mom. He carries her into the house, as he hollers, "Marilynn! Come in and help me get this bloody shirt off your mother. Joellen and D'Nelle! Get Deanne, Mike, and Danny to bed. Skeet! Skeet! I need you to help me with Jo Eva."

Everyone runs to do his or her assigned task. I stand beside the open car door and stare at the blood and tears on the floor of the driver's side; I don't know which is mine and which is Mom's. I don't know how we made it home. Tears roll down my cheeks. The numbness has worn off my gums, and my new braces feel like they are wired to the roof of my mouth. The inside of my upper lip sticks to the metal rods of the braces. Getting a straightened front tooth may not be worth all this.

I go into the house, change my clothes, and get into my bed. Joellen and I can't sleep; probably no one is sleeping, except Mike and Danny. When Marilynn tiptoes into the bedroom later that night, I ask her how Mom is doing.

Marilynn crawls under her thin cover and says, "She's in a lot of pain. The pills Dr. Love gave you don't seem to work much, maybe because she keeps throwing them up. She's just lying on her back, rolling her head from side to side. I guess that makes her feel better. Dad and Granddad are going to take turns sitting beside her. Granddad's a white as a ghost. He's holding Mom's hand and telling her she's a brave little girl. I think he's really lost his marbles this time. What happened in Dr. Love's office?"

I have trouble talking without my new braces sticking to my lips. "Dr. Love said he's getting her mouth ready for new teeth, so he had to pull all of the old teeth. That pink mold will help him make the new teeth."

Joellen turns on to her stomach and waves her feet around in the air. "Why can't Mom just use Granddad's false teeth? He never uses them. When did the dentist pull all of Granddad's teeth?"

Marilynn turns onto her side and acts like she is getting ready to go to sleep. "What makes you think a dentist pulled Granddad's teeth? Maybe somebody knocked them out."

Joellen twists her body around so that she can look at me. "Did Dr. Love give you all of the old teeth?"

I think that's a stupid question. "No."

Joellen turns on her back and gets ready to go to sleep. "Just think how much money she'd get from the tooth fairy. That would make her feel better."

I think Joellen will believe in the tooth fairy when she's a hundred years old.

PART III

Navajo Taboo: Do not look at your mother-in-law or speak to her because you will go blind or have trouble.

o o o o o o o o o o o o o o o o o o o o o o o o o o o o o o o o o

John F. Kennedy becomes the new president-elect.

President Eisenhower declares the Navajo reservation a disaster area following a severe drought.

7

Uvalde, Texas, 1960

Dr. Love's pain pills eventually work, and Mom manages to make it through the week by staying in bed with her head wedged between two pillows. The following week, she and I drive back to Cortez, where Dr. Love takes a little hammer and taps on the pink foam until it falls out of Mom's mouth. He declares, "Perfect."

Mom mumbles something, but we can't understand her because she is now toothless, just like Granddad. This time, Mom can drive home without my help. After a week of being toothless, Mom and I drive to Cortez again, where Mom gets her new teeth. She looks magnificent. Dr. Love creates a set of false teeth that look almost like her old teeth, except that they are all white and not spotty and gray. I watch Mom look at herself in the mirror in Dr. Love's office, and I think Mom's cheeks might explode from the smile plastered across her face.

Mom's new smile stays on her face as we prepare for our first visit to Texas since Grandma died. We are driving to Uvalde so that Dad can play in the Fourth of July golf tournament. I was born in Uvalde, and so were Marilynn, D'Nelle, Mom, Grandma, and Mammy (Grandma's mom). Grandma and Granddad lived in Uvalde before they moved to Farmington. I remember that Granddad said that he liked Uvalde because the white people have their own stores and the Mexicans have their own stores. In Uvalde, the Mexican kids go to their own school, and the white kids go to their own school. I think that Granddad would be happier if in our house, the white people had their own bedroom, and the Indians had a separate bedroom all to themselves.

Granddad moved to Texas when he was ten years old. Granddad, his dad, two brothers, two half brothers, and a half sister rode on a train from Kansas City, Missouri, to Sabinal, Texas. Granddad says that no one talked to injuns or Mexicans when he was a kid, so he doesn't see any reason to do it now. He says there is no reason to talk to an Indian or to live with Indians; he thinks Mom has gone a little crazy. I think Granddad just hasn't been around Mike and Danny long enough to learn to like them. Just because he didn't like Indians when he lived in

Texas doesn't mean he can't like them now. When we visit Texas, he's going to stay with Aunt Betty so he doesn't have to ride in the car with Mike and Danny, but he'll have to ride in the car with them for one day on our way to Texas and for one day on our way home from Texas. He's going to sit in the front, where he can't see the rest of us!

In Uvalde we will see Dad's mom and dad. Everyone calls Dad's mom "Big Mama." She is shorter than I am and about six times as wide. Dad's dad doesn't like it when we call him Granddad; he likes to be called "J. W.," which is short for Joseph Webster. He is a barber, and he has a smile and blue eyes that are even brighter than Dad's. J. W. also has a witching stick. Whenever we visit, he gets out his long, thin piece of willow that he calls a witching stick, and he lets us try to find water in his backyard. He tells us that we have to hold on to the end of the willow stick, and if there is water around, the stick will bounce up and down when we get near it.

Dad thinks I shouldn't wear my moccasins or concho belt to Texas; my tennis shoes and "regular white people clothes," as he calls them, is what he wants to see on my sisters and me. Bonnie told me that the Navajo word for white person is *bilagaana*. I can't pronounce it, but I understand that it probably means that I look funny in white people's clothes. On the day we leave, Dad hollers at me through my bedroom window, "And I don't want to hear any *ya'at'eeh*, either. Just say hello like a regular person."

Mike has learned how to use the toilet, so the only one in diapers is Danny. Mom plans to sit in the backseat near Danny, which means that Marilynn has to sit in the front seat between Dad and Granddad. Last night Dad drew up a diagram to help him figure out how to get ten people and Lady into the car, along with suitcases and Mom's ice chest full of Coca-Colas. Mom figures that because her new false teeth aren't real, she might as well keep drinking Cokes; she thinks nothing can hurt her new teeth. This morning Dad stands beside the car and stares at his diagram. He folds the two seats in the back of the station wagon flat and packs suitcases and pillows in the cracks to make one large flat area for Mom and my siblings and me to sit. He's ready to start placing bodies. "Marilynn or Joellen, one of you get out here and help me. Deanne, you're the first one in the car. so get out here!"

Dad steps in front of the car door and tries to block Lady from following Deanne into the car. Lady follows Deanne everywhere, and when she sneaks past Dad's waving arms, he yells at her, "No! Not Lady! Get that goddamn dog out of the car! It's not her turn." Dad calls into the house: "Mike! Danny! D'Nelle! Get out here, and wait beside the car until I tell you it's your turn. Jo Eva, are you ready? Joellen, put that ice chest behind my seat. Now let's put this last suitcase in behind Skeet's seat. Jo Eva, come on. We're waiting on you."

Mom rushes from the house with her arms full of bananas. She climbs in and sits behind Dad's seat.

Dad's elated. "Okay, D'Nelle, Mike, and Danny into the back. Lady, come, Lady! It's your turn. Skeet, you and Marilynn get in the front. Okay, Danalee, lock up the house and get out here."

I have the great honor of being the last one to squeeze into the back, sit cross-legged with my head bent, and try to keep Lady's breath out of my face. At least I get to sit by a window. I slowly walk through each room of the house and make sure the windows are locked and the water faucets are all turned off. I lock the door to the house and then climb in and close the car door. I hand Dad the key to the house, and Dad's car door slams. He talks to us over his shoulder. "Everybody cozy? Here we go."

The July heat outside the car is 105 degrees, and it's 115 degrees inside the car. My brothers and sisters and I are careful not to touch the interior metal parts of the car. Lady collapses; her tongue droops from her mouth. Mom sits right behind Dad's seat, with Danny and her ice chest full of Coca-Cola at hand. Joellen and D'Nelle occupy the back area, and Lady and Deanne and Mike claim the middle. I slide behind Granddad's seat and get my nose as close to the opened window as I can without sticking my whole head outside. Marilynn sits straight-backed and unmoving, with Dad on her left and Granddad on her right. Cigarette smoke swirls around her head.

Dad makes a bathroom stop every two hours whether we need it or not. The second bathroom stop is at a park, and we take a break for a picnic lunch. Mom and Marilynn get the food ready, and Joellen and I keep an eye on my sisters and brothers. An old man who sits on one of the park benches calls me a "nigger lover." I smile at him and pick up Danny and walk back to our table for lunch.

I ask Mom, "What's a nigger, and do we love them?"

She stares at me. "What?"

"A man called me a nigger lover, and I want to know what that is."

Mom looks me straight in the eye. "Nigger is not a nice word to use. Someone who has black skin is a Negro, not a nigger."

I still need to know. "Do you love them?"

Mom starts walking toward the car. "I certainly don't hate them."

Mom speeds up lunch and makes Mike and Danny sit in the car to eat. We are on the road again in record time and heading toward Aunt Betty's house. Aunt Betty lives in a prison. Uncle Bob is a prison guard, and Aunt Betty and my three cousins live in a gray house on the grounds of the state prison. At Grandma's funeral, my cousin told me that the school bus stops at the prison's gate each morning and picks up the kids who live at the prison.

It's late when we arrive, and Dad stops the car by a brightly lit electrical gate. A prison guard sprays his flashlight into the car. The beam of light passes from my face to my mom's to Danny's—and then stops. The light examines Dad's face, Marilynn's face, Granddad's face, and then my face, Mom's face, and Danny's face again. I watch the guard and think that if he's trying to count us, he's pretty slow—seven kids, three adults, and a dog; it's not that hard. The beam of light examines the rest of the faces in the car and then returns to Mike and Danny. The stern-faced guard slowly walks back to Dad's side of the car. He raises the metal arm blocking the entrance and waves us through.

A few minutes later we park before my aunt's gray house. Aunt Betty is waiting for us outside in the cool night air. She is as skinny as Granddad and prettier than Mom. Before any of us can get out of the car, she pokes her head in my window and says, "My, Jo Eva, don't y'all have a car full." She stands on her tiptoes and kisses Granddad on his cheek and allows him to pass into the house.

I watch him closely. Granddad has acted weird the whole week, and I'm afraid that he's going to throw a fit or something. Mom had to pack his suitcase for him. She made a little calendar with the exact number of days we'd be gone, when we'd drop him off, and when we'd pick him up. He seems okay now.

Aunt Betty prevents me from following Granddad into the house. She wraps her sweater around her shoulders and says, "Jo Eva, I've fixed up a special place for the rest of you. There's not really enough space in the house for everyone to stay."

I don't understand what she's talking about. We've stayed with Aunt Betty before, and she's always let my sisters and me sleep on the floors of my cousins' bedrooms. It's never been too crowded before.

Aunt Betty leads us through a small gate in the chain-link fence, up a darkened stairway, and into an old prisoners bunkhouse. A single, bare bulb illuminates the long, narrow room that is about as big as my classroom. Cockroaches scramble for cover when the dim light hits the wooden floor. The floor has been swept, but that is about all. Spiders try to hide in the weathered rafters of the ceiling. The bulb's dull light shines off the metal bars that cover the room's windows.

Permanently latched shutters prevent the cool night air from offering any relief to the room's heat. The one unshuttered window gives me a clear view of the prison's guard tower. Two guards, with rifles, stare down on us.

Nine metal cots with gray prison linen on the mattresses stand in a neat row against the room's back wall. Nine gray-striped pillows, without pillowcases, perch awkwardly on the mattresses.

Aunt Betty smiles and tells us, "This old prisoners barracks hasn't been used in years. There will be plenty of room for you here, and it's just a short walk over to my house. I'm sure you will be more comfortable here. Walk over in the morning when you're ready for breakfast. There's a toilet at the end of the room. Good night." She leaves without looking at Mom's new teeth, my new braces, or my new brothers.

In the morning Dad drives ten miles into Las Cruces to play golf; he needs some practice for the tournament. Mom and Marilynn help my brothers get dressed, and Deanne and D'Nelle try to catch the spider that lives in the corner of the old prisoners barracks. I didn't sleep much on account of the spiders watching me. Mom doesn't care if I'm sleepy or not; she wants Joellen and me to carry Mike and Danny over to Aunt Betty's house for breakfast. Mom says we have to carry them so their shoes don't get dirty, which will help us to keep Aunt Betty's floors clean. At age two, Mike looks like he could be a four-year-old, and he weighs a ton. Joellen carries Danny and promises to carry Mike on the way back to the barracks.

Joellen and I step through the front door of Aunt Betty's home and greet my three cousins. Aunt Betty hurries us into the kitchen, where Granddad sits sipping his morning coffee. He ignores Mike and Danny. "Morning, girls. Sleep well?"

Joellen and I stare at each other. We haven't been greeted like this in all the time that Granddad has lived with us. I set Mike down before I drop him, and he heads straight for the cat's bowl of food that is sitting by the back door. Danny won't let go of Joellen's neck, so she can't set him on the floor. Before I can stop Mike from eating the cat food, Aunt Betty sweeps by Granddad and places the bowls of breakfast cereal she has prepared for my brothers on the floor, next to the cat's dish. Mom enters the room at that moment and immediately grabs the bowls of cereal and puts them on the table, next to Granddad. Joellen holds Danny in her lap and feeds him. Mike takes a couple more tastes of the cat food before Mom can pick him up and sit him at the table. I stand beside his chair so that he won't fall out while he eats his cereal.

Aunt Betty turns her nose up at Mom and calls Mike and Danny dirty heathens. "Eating cat food. Disgusting."

By the time Dad returns from playing twenty-seven holes of golf, Mom and Aunt Betty have had enough of each other. It's funny to watch two grown-up sisters fight. Mom makes all of us get into the car while Dad thanks Aunt Betty for her hospitality. We drive an hour to Mammy's house in El Paso, where we will have dinner. I'm jealous of Mammy. She can visit Grandma's grave every day. Mom promises that I can visit Grandma's grave in the morning, before we leave for Uvalde.

Mammy's real name is Eve Ella Cantrell Weaver Gates. Mom is named after her—Jo Eva. Mom says Mammy is "real Texas blue blood." Her daddy moved to Texas when Indians still lived there. Mom tried to explain it to me once: "Eve Ella's father, George Washington Cantrell, married Sarah Louise Milan in 1855 and settled in the Uvalde area. He became one of the first beekeepers in Uvalde and contributed to Uvalde's becoming known as the honey capital of the world." She then squeezes my cheeks and says, "You're a little Texas honey."

I didn't know Uvalde was the honey capital of the world, and I can't imagine Mammy having a daddy that old. I can't imagine Mammy being Grandma's mother; she's just too polite and sugary, and besides, she looks old. I can see why Grandma ran away from home when she was sixteen years old to marry Grand-dad.

Everybody says that Mammy's never recovered from the time Grandma's younger brother died. One day, when he was just twenty-three, young Wade grabbed his chest, fell to his knees on the steps of the church, and keeled over and died. Grandma never went to church after that, and Mammy had to be happy with just Grandma and Grandma's sister, Sallie, for kids. Maybe that's why Mom has so many kids, in case one of us keels over one day and dies.

Mom says Mammy's mom grew up being polite to Indians so they wouldn't burn down her house, and so Mom thinks that Mammy will be nice to Mike and Danny. Mom says Mammy is making a big supper for us. Mom is overly worried about how we will behave, so she spends the hour it takes us to get there giving us all kinds of rules to follow when we arrive at Mammy's house. The rules for Mammy's house are:

1. Wipe your feet at the front door.

2. Shake Mammy's hand and say, "Thank you for having us to supper."

3. Don't touch anything in Mammy's living room.

4. Sit where Mammy tells you to at the supper table.

5. Eat everything put on your plate.

6. Don't ask for seconds.

7. Marilynn's job is to hold on to Mike at all times, and Joellen's job is to hold on to Danny at all times. Joellen gets a bottle of milk to help keep Danny quiet. Marilynn gets a loaf of bread to help keep Mike quiet.

8. My job is to make sure D'Nelle and Deanne follow the rules.

9. We have to say "Thank you" and "No, thank you" or Mom will wash out our mouths with soap.

Mammy is excited to see all of us. She wears a high-necked, gingham dress that clings to her small waist and delicate wrists. The straight seams of her dark support stockings line the backs of her skinny legs. Her pointy-framed glasses, just like the ones Grandma used to wear, never slip down her perfect nose.

At the doorway my sisters and I hug her and say, "Thank you for having us to supper." We march straight to the bathroom and wash our hands and then march directly into her tidy dining room. Mammy stands at the head of the table and says, "Marilynn, you and young Michael may sit beside me." She then points to the other side of the table. "Joellen, you and baby Daniel may sit over there." She continues issuing directives until we are all seated. Dad gets to sit at the opposite end of the dining table from Mammy because he is the dad.

So that there will be enough food to go around, Mom dishes up the food and won't let us help ourselves. Everyone gets one small scoop of mashed potatoes, one half slice of meatloaf, three green beans, and one half of a canned peach. The china water glasses that sit at the top of our china plates are filled with lukewarm milk. I'm as nervous as hell that I'm gonna spill something on my nice white lace napkin. For dessert we each receive one half slice of white bread that is buttered from corner to corner and lightly sugared—it's the best part of supper.

We didn't need Mom's rule about not touching anything in Mammy's living room, because after supper we thank Mammy for the wonderful supper and march straight to the car and leave. We drive like mad to my great-aunt Sallie's house, Grandma's younger sister. Sallie has a real supper ready for us, spaghetti and meatballs, applesauce, and chocolate cake for dessert. Grandma's sister can cook just as good as Grandma.

Our third day in the car is our last and our longest. Mom and Dad don't stop for a picnic; Mom hands out peanut better and jelly sandwiches and bananas, and we eat and ride at the same time. Bathroom stops are as fast as Dad can make them. At our bathroom stops, Dad carries Mike in to the men's bathroom, and Mom stays in the car with Danny until Dad and Mike return; then Mom runs to the bathroom. Sometimes when we are stopped at a red light, people stare into our car, but Mom tells us to just ignore stares. Shortly before suppertime, we pull into the driveway of Big Mama and J. W.'s tiny house that sits on the outskirts of Uvalde.

The brake is hardly in place before Dad jumps out of the car and hugs Big Mama. It's been over two years since he last saw his mom, and he's excited to be here. Big Mama can't get enough of Dad's hug. Dad has to bend over to hug her; she's not much taller than I am. She's square, like a box, and Dad's arms are just barely long enough to reach around her thick body. By the time they are through hugging, we are all standing on the driveway, waiting for our hugs. Big Mama gives long, smothery hugs. She smells like snicker-doodle cookie dough, cinnamon, and fresh lemons. She hugs my sisters and me and then Mom. Mom holds up Mike so Big Mama can meet him and give him a hug, but Big Mama only smiles and reaches out and barely touches his hand. "My, what a big boy you are," she says. She turns back to Marilynn, who is now holding Danny. "He's just a sweetheart." She doesn't touch his hand or hug him.

J. W. shadows Big Mama and shows us all his giant smile and blue, blue eyes. He hugs my sisters and me and tickles Mike and Danny on their tummies. Big Mama leads us toward the gate to the backyard and talks to Mom as she walks. "Jo Eva, I've made beds for the children in the garage and put some toys out there for them to play with. There is just not enough room in the house for all of the children and you and Joe. They will be safe out here with the gate locked and Marilynn and Joellen to keep an eye on them."

I watch Mom think about her reply. We are only staying at Big Mama's house for two days and then we are driving to Camp Wood to stay with Dad's older brother, Uncle Bubba. I know Mom is not going to fight about this. She smiles to Big Mama. "Why thank you, Big Mama. This will be just fine. They'll just come in the house to use the bathroom and to eat."

Big Mama has other plans. "Oh, J. W. set up a table for them in the yard, but I suppose they will have to come in the house to use the bathroom." Big Mama opens the gate to her small backyard and smiles to us. "Children, there is some milk and cookies for you on the table over there. We will have some supper soon, so don't ruin your appetites."

I think to myself that I'd like to see someone try to ruin Mike's appetite. My siblings and I settle into our temporary home in Big Mama's backyard. The garage closet is stuffed with toys, and the table under the shady pecan tree has an endless supply of snicker-doodle cookies.

That night, after Big Mama and Mom say their good nights, Marilynn, Joellen, and I drag all of the blankets and sleeping bags out of the hot, stuffy garage and onto the cool grass of Big Mama's backyard. We fall asleep to the sound of crickets and the twinkling of stars. Mike wakes up in the early morning hours and needs to go to the bathroom. Marilynn doesn't want to wake anyone in the house, so she lets him pee on the rose bushes; he thinks this is really funny.

The next morning we shove all of the sleeping gear back into the hot garage and wait at the table for our cereal and milk. We hear Mom and Dad arguing as they stand in the driveway beside the car. From the tone of his voice, we can tell that Dad is upset with Mom. "I need to get to the course. It's nearly time for the tournament. You can visit your—"

"The hell I can!" Mom interrupts. "I'm not staying in this house all day long with your mother. She'd just as soon spit at me as look at me. I'll drop you at the course and pick you up later. Now give me the goddamn car keys."

Marilynn, Joellen, and I eat our cereal in silence. We already know what will happen. Dad and Mom will leave, and the three of us will take turns changing Danny's diapers and listening to Big Mama tell us what a shame it was that her son married Jo Eva. From previous visits, we have the story memorized. Big Mama doesn't like Mom because she thinks Mom ruined Dad's chances of being a big golf star. She also thinks Dad shouldn't have married Mom because Grand-dad and Grandma were poor. Now, personally, I don't see how Granddad and Grandma's being poor can be Mom's fault. Dad always says that he fell in love with Mom because she looked so darn pretty on the dance floor. Mom always says that she fell in love with Dad because he looked so darn handsome in his Marine uniform.

It's too bad that Big Mama doesn't like Mom, but at least Mom knows it and is smart enough to spend the day somewhere else. We don't have the choice to spend the day somewhere else and besides, there are lots of toys in Big Mama's garage. After Danny and Mike wake up from their afternoon naps, Marilynn decides to take all of us for a walk to the Piggly Wiggly grocery store. The store is only about six blocks from Big Mama's house, and at age twelve, Marilynn is strong enough to carry Mike that far. Joellen is ten now, and she's been carrying Danny around for months. I'm really tall for nine, so I look older than Joellen. I hold D'Nelle's and Deanne's hands when we set out for the store. I have the hardest job because Deanne wants to run ahead of us and be the first one there. Lady barks at us for leaving her behind. Big Mama waves to us from the front porch and wipes her hands on her apron as if she's happy to get rid of us for a while.

When we reach the Piggly Wiggly, Marilynn walks about three feet into the store with Joellen on her heels when a man behind the counter looks up at her and yells, "This is a whites-only store, girls. Get those injuns out of here."

Marilynn's face turns as red as a beet as she and Joellen back out of the store. She deposits Mike on the sidewalk beside the rest of us and orders us to stay put until she returns. She then goes back into the store and reappears a few minutes later with seven red Tootsie Roll Pops. We wander up and down the sidewalk and wonder which is a whites-only store and which store is for Mexicans. I wonder if Indians are allowed to go into the Mexicans-only store, or if there is a store for Indians only. I wonder why the store's owner doesn't just put a sign in the window of the store: "whites only" or "Indians only."

We don't see any signs in windows, and we can't figure out just by looking at the front of the store whether or not Mike and Danny can go inside, so we head back to Big Mama's backyard and play with the toys from the closet in the garage.

That night we pull the bedding out into the yard again, and when the four youngest are asleep, Big Mama sticks her head out of the kitchen door and calls Marilynn and Joellen inside to watch television. When the kitchen door closes, I pull the sheet over my head and shine the flashlight onto the pages of the book I am reading. At times like this I wish Big Mama liked me as much as she likes Marilynn and Joellen.

On our last day at Big Mama's, while we pack the car and get ready to drive to Uncle Bubba's house, Big Mama tries to help Dad understand what a bad influence Mom is on him. As he puts the last suitcase into the car, she slides her big square body up next to his and says in a quiet voice, "Joe Daniel, what are you thinking? Jo Eva has made you do a bad thing."

Big Mama thinks we can't hear her, but she's wrong. We are all standing beside the car, waiting to climb in. Dad turns to face her. "Mama." Dad never calls his mom Big Mama. "Mama, Mike and Danny are my sons. Jo didn't make me do anything. If you don't want us to stay with you next time we come, we have plenty of other places to stay, but I wish you'd accept Mike and Danny. They're your grandsons."

Big Mama can see she's not persuading Dad and tries again in a louder voice. "But Joe Daniel, this is not a good thing. Indians should live with Indians."

Before Big Mama can continue, Mom walks over to Dad and puts her arm around his shoulder and pulls him away from Big Mama. "Come on, honey, let's get going."

I smile to myself as I climb into the car. Mom hasn't called Dad "honey" in a really long time. We all wave good-bye to Big Mama and J. W. as the car pulls away from their tiny white house.

The drive to Uncle Bubba's takes less than an hour. Camp Wood is a very small town, with two stores surrounded by lots of sheep ranches. Uncle Bubba and Aunt Grace raise sheep. When we visit during the summer, we get to see the sheep without their wooly coats. Uncle Bubba and Aunt Grace both have wrinkly skin, and they both smoke more cigarettes in one day than Dad does in a week. Sometimes I can barely see their faces through the cigarette smoke.

After a round of hugs and kisses with Uncle Bubba and Aunt Grace, Mom settles the boys down for a nap in the spare bedroom. D'Nelle and Deanne help Aunt Grace make cookies. Uncle Bubba has a special project for Marilynn, Joellen, and me—he's going to teach us how to shoot a gun. He tells Mom, "You never know when they might need to protect themselves. Having injuns for brothers is a dangerous thing."

Mom tells him to hush up, but Uncle Bubba goes straight into his house and comes out with a gun and a box of shells.

Mom pushes Dad in the back. "Joe Daniel, stop this nonsense right now. Go tell Bubba to put that gun away."

Dad grabs his putter from the car and starts to practice his stroke. He doesn't seem too worried about his big brother teaching us how to shoot a gun. "Aw, it won't hurt them to learn how to shoot a gun. Bubba taught me how to shoot when I was about Danalee's age. Just relax."

As I follow Uncle Bubba toward the barn, I watch Mom stomp down the steps of the front porch and grab the putter out of Dad's hands. "I will not 'just relax'! March down to the barn right this minute and bring back my girls."

The last thing I hear as I round the corner of the house on my way to the barn is Dad calmly replying, "Now, Jo, go get yourself a Coke and sit down and read a book. I'm not going to the barn and neither are you."

The tall grass that lines the path to the barn scratches my legs. I'm the last in line, as always, and Marilynn's in the lead. I scratch my legs and complain at the same time. "Uncle Bubba, it's too hot to shoot a gun."

Uncle Bubba doesn't break his stride. He puffs on his cigarette and says, "Nonsense."

Sheep occupy the big pen outside the barn doors. Four-month-old lambs run to the fence to see why we are there. Uncle Bubba's dog, Rusty, barks at the sheep and then runs circles around Uncle Bubba and wags his tail.

When we reach the back of the barn, he hands me some empty tin cans. "Run and put these tin cans on the top rail of the fence down by those oak trees, and then get back up here and stuff these cotton balls in your ears or you'll go deaf."

I run to the fence with the empty tin cans, thinking, *Deaf! Deaf! I don't want to go deaf. I don't want to learn to shoot a gun. I want to go back to the house and read my book.*

Joellen and I stay behind Marilynn when Uncle Bubba puts a pistol in her right hand and says, "Here, Marilynn, show them how to do it. Straighten your arm, look down the barrel of the gun, and when you see the tin can, squeeze the trigger."

Uncle Bubba stands back, grins, and watches Marilynn squint her left eye and stare down the barrel of the gun with her right. The heavy gun wavers in her right hand, but she manages to squeeze the trigger. Her right arm flies upward and she steps back. The tin cans are all safe.

I inch closer to Joellen's back and whisper, "Where did the bullet go."

Joellen shrugs her shoulders. "Beats me. Maybe it keeps going until it hits something."

Uncle Bubba continues to throw all of his attention on Marilynn. "Try it again. Hold the gun steady."

Marilynn bites her lower lip and tries again. The gun discharges and once again the tin cans remain on the top rail of the fence. Marilynn lowers the gun, stomps her right foot into the dirt, and mumbles, "Shit."

I try not to smile. I've finally found something Marilynn's not good at.

Uncle Bubba gives up on Marilynn, takes the gun from her hand, and turns to Joellen. "Joellen. You give it a try."

Joellen replaces Marilynn, who stomps over to the sheep pen and chews her fingernails. Joellen holds the gun steady with her right arm, straightens her arm, and looks down the barrel of the gun. Uncle Bubba is excited again. "Fire when you think you can hit a can."

Uncle Bubba doesn't know that Joellen doesn't think she can ever hit a can, and she doesn't look down the barrel of the gun before she fires. The first can on the fence post plummets to the ground. An astonished Marilynn grumbles to herself, "Beginner's luck."

Joellen turns and smiles at Marilynn. She raises the gun, doesn't bother to look down the barrel again, and pulls the trigger. Two cans fall from the fence's railing. Marilynn pounds her feet into the dirt and exclaims, "Shit. Shit. Shit!"

Joellen grins and flips the gun around and hands it, handle first, to me. She moves and aside and says, "Your turn."

I feel Marilynn's eyes boring though the back of my head. Uncle Bubba gives me the same speech that he gave Marilynn and Joellen. "Keep your arm straight. Look down the barrel of the gun and squeeze the trigger." He reminds me, "You might be the one they'll go after. You'd better learn to shoot."

I smile at Uncle Bubba; I'm pretty sure no one is going to "go after" me because I have two Indians for brothers. I would like to shoot a can off the fence, but I can barely hold the gun up in front of me—it's heavy—and my other problem is that because Mom won't buy me glasses, I can barely see the tin cans sitting on the rail.

I lean closer to Joellen and whisper, "Joellen. Joellen. I can't see the cans. Everything in front of me is all blurry."

Joellen stands directly behind me and says, "Shoot what you can see. What can you see?"

I stare down the barrel of the gun and tell her, "I can see Uncle Bubba."

Joellen reaches around and lowers my gun arm. "Don't shoot him! Aim the gun toward the fence. I'll say up or down and right or left. Ready?"

This sounds like it might work, as long as Uncle Bubba stays behind me. I tell her I'm ready. Marilynn is tired of watching Joellen and me and says in a frustrated voice, "Oh, for Christ's sake, stop being a chicken and shoot the fucking gun."

Uncle Bubba stares at Marilynn and smiles. "I see you're taking after your dad."

I'm not a champion gunslinger like Joellen. I can't hit a can that I can't see. The fence, the cans, and the trees are one big cloudy mess. Tears hang in the bottom of my eyes as I aim the gun, stare down the barrel, and pull the trigger. Joellen informs me that all of the tin cans remain on the rail.

Uncle Bubba grabs the gun from my shaking hand and says, "Okay. That's enough for today. Maybe you can try again when your mom buys you some glasses. Looks like you need some."

The four of us tromp back through the tall grass to Uncle Bubba's porch, where Mom grabs each of us and smothers us in kisses as if we'd been away for a month.

That night I lie on the cool floor of the porch and listen to the sounds of sleep. Earlier, Aunt Grace made us a big pot of lamb stew and cornbread with honey. She promised me that I could have cornbread and honey for breakfast. Mom and Dad and my brothers share the spare bedroom, and my sisters and I share the porch. The sheet is pulled over my head and tucked in all around me in an attempt to keep mosquitoes off of me. The slow, measured breathing of my sisters tells me that I am the only one fighting off the mosquitoes.

I think of Uncle Bubba's desire to teach us how to shoot a gun. Will I really need to protect myself and Mike and Danny? What is so bad about having Indians for brothers? I don't understand. No one in Shiprock seems to think it is a bad thing to have Indians for brothers. Maybe we should just stay in Shiprock and not visit Big Mama and Uncle Bubba.

Our one-day stay at Uncle Bubba's house is amazing. Mike and Danny get to touch a lamb. We all go down to the sheep pen and try counting sheep to see if we will fall asleep, but no one does. Danny takes his first steps on the old wooden porch of Uncle Bubba's house. Aunt Grace is so excited that she coughs and coughs and coughs until she cries. Mom and Dad kid around with each other and Dad chases her around the front yard while she laughs. It's fun being at Uncle Bubba's house, but I am ready to go home and see my friends.

Dad drives toward El Paso, our first stop on our way home. At lunchtime we stop at a roadside diner, and we all follow Dad into the restaurant. As we walk through the screen door of the diner, a tall man with a baseball cap on his head and a dirty apron around his waist points to Dad and says in a loud voice, "Hey, you. Hey, you—with the golf cap on! Those Indians will have to wait outside." The man holds a greasy spatula in the air as he stares at Dad.

Mom can't believe that the man seriously means what he says. "But they're just babies."

The man stares at her and shrugs his shoulders. "I don't care how old they are. They're Indians. Get 'em out of my restaurant."

Mom hands Danny to Joellen, as Dad hands Mike to Mom. We leave the restaurant and wait for Dad in the car. Dad soon returns with nine hamburgers. I sit in the car with my uneaten hamburger in my lap and think about the angry face of the man in the restaurant.

I'm sick of Texas. I'm beginning to understand why Mike and Danny can't go in the stores in Uvalde or eat at a restaurant—everybody in Texas is just like Granddad. I wonder if Uncle Bubba believes that my knowing how to shoot a gun will prevent people from acting like Granddad. My hamburger sits untouched on my lap while I try to figure out what's bad about being an Indian. Dad isn't eating his hamburger, either; his face has become like steel. Mom cradles Danny in her arms as tears slowly trickle down her face. She watches Mike joyfully stuff his hamburger into his mouth. It's hard not to smile when watching Mike; he loves everything. I wonder if he'll love not being able to go into the stores in Uvalde each time we visit.

Several hours later we collect Granddad from Aunt Betty's house, make a fast bathroom stop, and continue driving. Dad and Granddad take turns driving until we reach Shiprock. In the early hours of the morning, when Granddad is driving, I lean my back against the passenger seat and listen to Dad and Granddad whisper to each other. Granddad is like a child, wanting to play a game of "I told you so." He chuckles and whispers, "Well, Joe, what did your folks think about your boys?" If it was light outside, I'm sure I would see Granddad smiling. Dad doesn't answer. Granddad tries another way to irritate Dad. "What're you going to do with those boys when they get to be Marilynn's age, and they bring little injun girls home for your approval?"

Dad scoots lower into the passenger seat and gets ready to sleep. He turns to Granddad and says, "Skeet, I don't know what the hell will happen in the future and neither do you. Just shut up and drive."

I don't know what will happen in the future, either, but I'm beginning to worry that it won't all be fun. I don't see anything wrong with Mike and Danny bringing home a Navajo girlfriend. When I'm old enough, I'm going to bring home a Navajo boyfriend.

8

Shiprock, 1960

When we return to Shiprock, I'm happy that the trading post doesn't have a sign in the window reading "White people—stay out." Nothing much changed while we were gone. Bonnie and her siblings attended Vacation Bible School all summer. Her dad doesn't have a church of his own, so the church meets in the auditorium of the junior high school. Next summer I don't want to go to Uvalde; I want to stay with Bonnie and go to Vacation Bible School.

Bonnie and I have the same teacher this year. Mrs. Thomas's third-grade classroom is a small heaven. Mrs. Thomas might be older than my great-grandma, Mammy, but no one would ever know it. Before school starts each year, she scrubs every inch of her classroom, and then she repaints the walls and sands and restains the wooden desktops. Each year, everything in Mrs. Thomas's classroom is new, just for her students.

The back corner of the classroom is a lending library. The bookmobile only stops in Shiprock once a month, but I learn that if I need more books, I can borrow a book from Mrs. Thomas' lending library. She has books I've never heard of—*Robinson Crusoe, Moby Dick,* and *Treasure Island.* This is the best classroom I've ever had. The school year starts perfectly—but perfect doesn't last very long. Polio spreads through the reservation, along with rheumatic fever and tuberculosis. All of the children in my school, the mission school, and the boarding school have to get polio vaccinations. If the mom or dad can get the school kids' younger siblings to school, they can also get a shot. Mike and Danny get one.

The cafeteria's line of children snakes across the wide room and into the school's hallway. The new school nurse smiles at each student and then jabs a needle into his arm. She's worked her way through the first and second graders, and now the students in my class face her. I repeat to myself as I stand in line behind Bonnie, "I won't be a chicken. I won't be a chicken. I won't be a chicken."

Each student in front of me holds up the shirt sleeve of his left arm and looks to the right as the nurse jabs the long thin needle into his arm. Third graders are brave. I get closer and closer to the head of the line and repeat to myself, faster and faster, "I won't be a chicken. I won't be a chicken."

Bonnie, standing in front of me, gets her shot and then turns to wait for me. She shakes my arm and says, "What's the matter with you? You're all white."

The nurse starts to give me the shot, but she stops the needle in midair. "Honey, are you all right?" she asks.

My skin turns icy cold. The nurse's face blurs before me, and I hear her yelling, "Somebody help me!" My knees buckle, and I fall to the cool linoleum floor of the cafeteria.

My fainting spell is the talk of the school. I will die of embarrassment—if Marilynn doesn't kill me first. That night in bed, with the covers pulled up over my head, Joellen defends my fainting spell to Marilynn. She stands by the side of the bed, reaches under the cover and places a cool, wet washcloth on my forehead. "She is not a chicken," Joellen says. "She has a little cold and standing in line made her sicker."

Marilynn busies herself by hanging a new magazine picture of Buz, from *Route 66,* on her wall. She smirks. "She's a chicken, and you know it. Can't even get a little shot."

Joellen flips the wet washcloth so that the cool side is on my forehead. "She is not."

Marilynn puts her hands on her hips. "She fainted and scared the new nurse so much that she's already quit her job."

"Oh, she didn't quit her job," Joellen huffs. "She ran away. She ran away with the lady who lives in Farmington."

Marilynn huffs right back. "Dummy, women don't run away together."

Joellen raises her eyebrows at Marilynn. "You're the dummy. Vicky told Mom that the nurse is a homo, and this was the only job she could find."

Marilynn looks at the picture on the wall. "You don't even know what a homo is."

Joellen is too smart to fall for that. "Neither do you."

Marilynn doesn't look in our direction. "I do, too."

"No, you don't," Joellen retorts.

I remove my head from the covers long enough to yell, "Oh, shut up! I was a chicken, and I scared the nurse so much she ran away. Now shut up and leave me alone!"

The arrival of the Navajo Fair in late September gives people something to talk about besides my fainting spell and the school nurse. Navajo families arrive for the Fair by flatbed wagons, pickup trucks, and on foot. Thick, black smoke from campfires settles in over Shiprock. The smell of cooked mutton and Navajo fry bread floats down the highway. It is difficult to concentrate on schoolwork when the activities of the Fair come to life.

Marilynn thinks that because she has lived in Shiprock for so long and because she has two Navajo brothers, it would be reasonable for her to dance in the Kinaaldá ceremony this year, along with her Navajo friends from school. This is a four-day ceremony for thirteen-year-old girls who have started their periods. It celebrates a transition into womanhood. Even though I know Marilynn has already started her period, she won't be thirteen for a few more months. Mom tries to explain that only Navajo girls are allowed to dance in the ceremony. She adds, "If someone has invited you to watch, then you should be happy. White people don't usually get to watch, so be happy with that."

Granddad's loud, angry voice interrupts. "Jo Eva, come get this injun away from me." From my bedroom window, I see Granddad sitting outside by the cottonwood tree. Danny, excited by his new ability to walk everywhere, repeatedly tries to walk up to Granddad and put his hand on Granddad's knee. Granddad repeatedly shoos him away. Danny thinks it's a game; Granddad does not.

Mom yells, "Danalee, go get your brother."

On the weekend before the Tribal Fair, Mom and Vicky dye each other's hair. Mom's new orange hair is supposed to be "sultry red." I think she looks great, but when Dad sees it, he is not too happy with the color. The first words out of his mouth are: "Jesus H. Christ! What the fuck have you done to your hair? You're not going to the Fair like that, are you?"

I watch tears form in the bottom of Mom's eyes as she tries to think of a response. Dad sees the tears too. He takes hold of her hand and says, "Well, hon, now that I take a closer look, it's not too bad. Maybe you could wear your big straw hat."

Mom's tears burst into a full-blown bawl, and she runs from the room and slams the door to their bedroom. Dad looks at me, but I just shrug my shoulders. Sometimes Mom just cries at the smallest thing.

At the Fair, Mom proudly holds Mike's hand and carries Danny around as if the boys wore first-prize blue ribbons around their necks. Orange hair sneaks out from under the brim of her big straw hat. Marilynn and Dad walk ahead of the rest of us, as if they don't know us.

I've never seen so many people. I wish I could dress like a Navajo all of the time—purple skirts, red blouses, knee-high moccasins, and lots and lots of jewelry. At least I have moccasins and a concho belt. I carry the small piece of turquoise that Vicky gave me two years ago in my pocket, along with two arrowheads that I found. Arrowheads are lucky like turquoise. Between the turquoise and arrowheads, nothing bad should happen to me. I've seen the coyote snooping around the garbage can tower. In the morning, I always try to figure out where he's walked so I won't cross his tracks, but the tracks are always mixed up with Lady's tracks, and I can't tell which tracks belong to which animal. Dad makes sure Lady stays in the house at night; he says the coyote might attack Lady, and we don't want that to happen. I wish the coyote would go and find another garbage can tower to snoop around.

With ten thousand people in town for the Fair, I bet the coyote is too afraid to snoop around. Each year when the Fair is in town, Shiprock becomes another world. The posters for the Fair read "Pale or Red, everyone is welcome." On the first day of the Fair there is a big parade, and each grade decorates a float. For weeks before the parade, we spend our time after school stuffing chicken wire with toilet tissue. Then the stuffed chicken wire is wrapped around an old pickup truck. The truck looks like a giant white flower rolling down the highway. The parade has high school marching bands. Shiprock doesn't have a high school yet; the students ride a bus to Kirkland. Horses march in the parade, and people have to follow the horses and scoop up the poop—it's great.

The Catholic mission across the highway from our house hosts a big dance on Friday and Saturday nights. During the day, people watch bareback riding, bull riding, calf roping, and barrel racing. For Joellen and me, the best part of the Fair is the Miss Navajo contest. This year's contest has changed to include a modern Miss Navajo. I figure that I might be able to enter this contest when I'm fifteen years old because I'm kind of like an honorary Navajo. Dad says that Mike and Danny are white because they now live with a white family, so I think I could be considered Navajo because I live in a partially Navajo family.

As Joellen and I walk along the dusty, makeshift path of the Fair, we are surrounded by rodeo events. A man sitting on top of a bull waves his arm in the air and then tumbles to the ground. I enjoy watching people try to throw a lasso around the skinny neck of a calf. Beautiful woven blankets thrown on the ground to my right hold silver and turquoise jewelry for sale. I can't afford any jewelry. Pickup trucks, with their tailgates down, are lined up beside the jewelry. From the tailgates, Navajo women sell fry bread and lamb stew. In the back of the pickups, ice chests hold jars of cool cow's milk for sale.

On the edge of the fairgrounds, the nine-day ceremony of the Night Chant, or *Yei Bi Cheii* begins; it includes the *Kinaaldá* dance. White people are not allowed to watch some parts of this ceremony, but I suspect that Marilynn will be glued to the area for the duration of the Fair. She wants to participate in the *Kinaaldá*, the dance that signifies that a Navajo girl is now a woman and eligible to marry. During this ceremony the Navajo women help the girls through the parts of the ceremony that signify the journey to womanhood. In the world of the Navajo, all adult women can be referred to as "mother," so one's sisters, aunts, and grandmothers may be called mother; everyone helps each other.

After watching the bull riders for a while, Joellen and I walk back up the highway to the Catholic mission, the site for the Miss Navajo contest. For the traditional category this year, the contestant wears traditional clothing, and she has to know how to spin and weave wool and how to prepare fry bread. She also has to tell a story in Navajo. I can't do any of those things. For the modern category, the contestant has to wear a modern dress, sew something, and speak English. When I learn how to sew I will be able to try out for Miss Navajo in the modern category. For now, I lose myself in the world of the Navajo and am thankful to be here.

The black haze that hangs over Shiprock disappears at the close of the Fair. The cowboys and Navajo women selling fry bread drive to some other rodeo, and I have to wait another whole year for the next Fair. Shiprock returns to normal but continues to grow. New houses line the highway, and more are being built. Sheep strolling down the middle of the highway now give way to more traffic. Halloween comes and goes. This year Mike and Danny trick-or-treat with us, and Mom makes Granddad stay in his room. Danny learns new words every day, and he and Mike are inseparable. Their favorite activity is sitting on the floor of the living room with a loaf of bread between them. They tear out the center of each slice and roll it into a small ball; then they eat them as fast as they can.

A few weeks before Christmas, after the snow and ice has settled in, Joellen and I are sitting in the backseat of the car. I hold her close to me in an effort to keep her warm. I watch Mom grip the steering wheel as the car skids across the frozen road. I'm afraid Mom's going to skid off of the road before we reach the hospital in Cortez. She can't drive as well as Dad, and she's already run over a rabbit and a raccoon.

Joellen's hands are cold and sticky and her head is on fire. She shivers even with the blanket Mom brought along and my coat on top of her. She's wearing two sweaters and two pair of pants, so she looks fatter than she really is. Her short brown hair sticks to her hot forehead. She hasn't been able to breathe for a week; she makes tiny whistles when she breathes in.

Mom tries to turn around to look at Joellen and drive at the same time. "How's she doing?"

I lean forward toward the front seat. I whisper, in case Joellen is asleep, "She's still cold. The coats and blanket aren't working."

Mom whispers back, "I've got the heater cranked up as far as it will go. Wrap your arms around her and hug her. We're almost there. The road is icy, so I have to drive slowly. You'll both get nice warm hospital beds when we get to Cortez."

I snuggle closer to Joellen and tuck the loose ends of the blanket around her. I stretch my arms wide and try to wrap my arms around her pudgy body. Joellen is my closest friend; I will do anything for her. She is the only person who can read my mind. She knows when to talk and when to shut up. Dad says we're two peas in a pod.

She leans her head against mine and whispers in a hoarse voice, "Danalee, I'm scared. What if I don't wake up after the doctor makes me go to sleep for the operation?"

I try to be as cheery as I can. "Oh, you'll be fine. The medicine the doctor gives you will only make you stay asleep for the operation. When you wake up, your tonsils will be gone, and you won't have a fever. And you can eat all the ice cream you want."

Joellen wants to believe me, but she's still scared. "And when you wake up from having your tonsils out, you can eat all of the ice cream you want, too. If the doctor wants you to get fatter, why doesn't he just give you some ice cream instead of taking out your tonsils? Why will taking your tonsils out make you get fat? Will I get fat when they take out my tonsils? Danny didn't get fat when they took out his tonsils."

I put my hand over her mouth and beg her, "Stop talking! I don't know why taking my tonsils out will make me fat. Mom says I won't be so skinny after they take out my tonsils. She doesn't want me to be skinny like Granddad. She wants me to look like you and Marilynn."

Joellen thinks hard and then whispers, "Hey, maybe they took out Marilynn's tonsils when she had rheumatic fever, 'cause she's getting kind of fat now."

Sometimes I wish Joellen were smarter than she is. "No, she's just getting older and fatter. I do know that she ate lots of ice cream when she stayed at the hospital, and now we get to eat as much ice cream as she did."

Joellen's voice is disappearing, but she still has things to say. "Danalee, is Dad mad at us for having our tonsils out?"

I know what she means. Dad is always worried about money, and when an emergency happens that requires money, he gets very quiet. I tell Joellen, "I don't think so. He just gets mad about paying bills."

Joellen sips water from the glass bottle we brought along. "Are we not going to have Christmas because Dad can't pay bills, like the year Grandma died? I hope we have Christmas this year. It's Danny's first Christmas with us."

Now Joellen has asked a question I can answer. "Last week, when Mom came home from buying groceries in Farmington, I saw her hide three boxes under her bed. That means that at least three of us are getting presents."

Joellen is temporarily distracted from her sore throat and the cold car. "Was it a big box?"

Before I can answer, Mom announces, "Here we are, girls. Just stay where you are, and a nurse will come to help Joellen out of the car."

Joellen clings to my arm when I try to take the blanket and coats off of her. She whispers frantically, "Danalee! You won't be a chicken, will you? You'll hold my hand the whole time, like you said you would?"

My heart pounds in my ears. Now I'm the one with cold, sticky hands. I close my eyes and say a silent prayer to Grandma:

Dear Grandma,

Please don't let me be a chicken.

I put my hand over Joellen's and swear, "I won't be a chicken. I'll be beside you the whole time. I'll tell them to bury our tonsils together."

Hours later, I hold Joellen's warm, dry hand and wait for her to wake up. From my bed in the hallway, I can see Mom and a nurse standing at the end of the long hallway. They are yelling at each other.

"Danalee? Why are we in the hall?" Joellen's tiny voice sounds strained and sore. She repeatedly sticks out her tongue, trying to find some moisture.

I place a wet washcloth over her lips and say, "There aren't enough rooms in the hospital. Lots of people are in the hallway."

Joellen stares at me as if I've betrayed her. She lowers the wet washcloth. "You're not hoarse. Did you chicken out and not have your tonsils removed?"

I sit up on my bed and reassure her. "No, they're gone. My throat is just not as sore as yours. Drink some more water."

Joellen is too tired to sit up. "Where's my ice cream?"

I've been dreading that question. I heard Mom and the nurse arguing earlier. I break the news to Joellen. "I don't think we're getting any ice cream. The nurse said there's no one to bring it up from the kitchen. Everyone at the hospital is really busy right now."

Joellen props herself up on her elbows. "Where's Mom?"

I point to the end of the hall. "She's talking to the nurse." Mom throws her nose in the air and stomps away from the nurse. "Well, it looks like she's leaving."

Joellen collapses onto her bed. "Leaving? Where's she going?"

I watch Mom try to slam the swinging door at the end of the hallway. I can't imagine where she is going. I lie down on my own bed and turn to Joellen. "How do I know?"

After a few minutes, Mom walks through the swinging doors with a large brown box in her hands. The red-faced nurse trails along behind Mom, yelling, "Wait a minute! You can't do this! Stop! I'll have to report you!"

Mom doesn't stop walking. "Go right ahead," she retorts. She stops at the first bed she comes to in the hallway. "Would you like some ice cream?" She sticks her hand in the brown box, smiles at the little boy in the bed, and hands him a small, round, plastic cup of vanilla ice cream and a tiny wooden spoon. Right and left, she walks down the wide hallway and hands out cups of ice cream until she reaches our beds. Mom tickles Joellen's feet and pats my leg. "Here you go, girls. Eat all the ice cream you want." She sets the brown box on the edge of my bed and turns to stare at the angry nurse.

The nurse stares back at Mom and then shakes her head and returns to what she was doing before Mom showed up with the box of ice cream. In the bottom of the box, the remaining cups of vanilla ice cream begin to melt. I hand Joellen two cups and a wooden spoon and take two for myself. The cool ice cream drips down my sore throat. When I get fatter, I wonder how the doctor will know if it was the tonsils or the ice cream that made me fat.

PART IV

Navajo Taboo: Do not stare at anyone for a long time or you will go blind.

o o o o o o o o o o o o o o o o o o o o o o o o o o o o o o

East Germany erects the Berlin Wall.

The reservation suffers the worst winter storm in recorded history; Shiprock temperatures plummet to -25 degrees.

9

Uvalde, 1961

Joellen and I celebrate New Year's Eve at home with our brothers and sisters and lots and lots of ice cream. On January 20, we listen to the sounds of President Kennedy's inaugural parade on the radio. The *Navajo Times* newspaper will have pictures of the Navajo marching band and float, but for now I can only close my eyes and imagine their knee-high moccasins and colorful uniforms. The Navajo men and women I know from the trading post are very happy that President Kennedy won the election. I ask Dad if he voted for President Kennedy, but he just shrugs his shoulders and says, "I never vote."

A week later, four thousand people descend on Shiprock for the dedication of the new police station and courthouse. The policemen have a parade and show off their new cars and uniforms, and then they get in a long, long line, and some-one from the *Navajo Times* takes their picture. The governor, Edwin Meehan, and the police commander, Captain James Smith, give speeches. The parade is the best part of the day.

Nothing exciting happens to me until the end of the school year, when I dis-cover that I will be in Mr. Schmidt's fourth-grade classroom next year, and I get my braces off. I am so excited to be in Mr. Schmidt's class. He has a happy face and a loud voice. I can hear his voice as he talks to his class when I'm sitting in Mrs. Thomas' class. Deanne is friends with Mr. Schmidt's daughter, and she is very quiet and nice, so I figure Mr. Schmidt also must be nice.

I'm sad, though, because I'll miss Mrs. Thomas. She talked to Mom about getting glasses for me so that I could see the chalkboard, but Mom just thanked her for her concern and didn't buy me glasses. We can't really afford it. When Joellen and I came home from the hospital, Mrs. Thomas brought me books from the lending library. I will miss her kind, sweet voice and her lending library.

I'm also sad because Dad is playing in the Uvalde Fourth of July golf tourna-ment this summer, so we will drive to Uvalde in a few weeks. In the meantime, I cross the highway to the junior high school each morning and go to Vacation

Bible School with Bonnie. In the afternoons I hide in the hole in the ground on the boarding school's playground; it is the only cool place in Shiprock to sit and read.

This afternoon D'Nelle hides with me. She twists a small stick into the smooth mud wall of the hole in the ground and nudges me in the arm. "Hey! Stop daydreaming and answer my question. What's a half-breed?"

I ignore her. The dirt walls of the hideout haven't changed in three years. I wonder what it would be like to hide in here and wait for someone to bring me food and water. Bonnie says some of the kids who live at the boarding school hide in this hole until they can sneak away and run back to their homes. It's hard enough living in a house with six brothers and sisters; I can't imagine having 999 roommates, like the kids in the boarding school. The children who live at the boarding school must like each other a lot.

D'Nelle nudges me again. "Come on, what's a half-breed?"

I keep reading my book, but then I answer her. "You know what it is. It's when someone has one parent who is white and one who is Indian. Sue and Bill, the kids who live in the Kerr-McGee compound, are half-breeds 'cause their mom is Indian and their dad is white."

D'Nelle stops twisting the stick and stares at me. "Sue's mom is an Indian?" D'Nelle's not finished with her questions. "How come Indians can't go in the store in Uvalde? I don't want to stay on the sidewalk with Mike and Danny this year. I want to go inside, like Marilynn."

I've thought about the prospect of standing on the sidewalk in Uvalde a lot since last summer. I don't want to stand on the sidewalk this summer, either. I try to help D'Nelle understand something that I don't fully understand. "I guess people in Uvalde are still afraid of Indians. When Mama Austin was a little girl, Indians still rode around on horses and burned white peoples' houses and killed them. Maybe the white people in Uvalde are still afraid of Indians."

D'Nelle's eyes grow wide. "Wow, I didn't know Mama Austin was that old."

D'Nelle is very good at math, so I tell her to figure it out. "Well, when Grand-dad was fourteen years old, his dad married Mabel, and Mabel is Mama Austin's daughter—that makes her Granddad's step-grandmother. Granddad was born in 1903, and Mama Austin is his grandmother so she was born before 1903, so she's really, really old. I'm glad we're staying at her house this summer, instead of sleeping in Big Mama's yard."

"Yeah, but we have to stay at Big Mama's for two days," D'Nelle reminds me, "so Dad can win the golf tournament."

I return to reading my book. "I know, but I don't have to like it."

The day we leave for Uvalde, Dad acts like one of his old Marine drill sergeants. He stands beside the car and yells, "Skeet, if you don't get in the car in the next five minutes, you can stay in Shiprock by yourself this summer."

I cram into my usual spot, right behind Granddad's seat. The car door is closed, and the windows are rolled down so that hot, dry air flows into the car's interior. D'Nelle sits in the back of the station wagon beside Lady and Deanne. We're waiting for Granddad to find his mandolin and get into the car so we can leave. While we wait, Lady and Deanne have a panting contest. Joellen, Mike, and Danny sit in the middle of the flat area in the back. Mom gives Mike and Danny a loaf of bread to munch on while we wait for Granddad.

Marilynn sits on the front seat, pouting, because Mom and Dad won't let her stay in Shiprock by herself this summer; she thinks she's old enough. Mom sits behind Dad's seat, with her opened bottle of Coke shoved under her nose; she uses it like smelling salts. Dad stands by his opened car door and practices imaginary golf swings. I wonder what would happen if Dad lost a golf tournament.

I'm just as anxious as Dad to get going. This summer we only have to camp in Big Mama's backyard for two days, then we're going to Mama Austin's house on the Frio River in Leakey, about an hour away from Uvalde. I think she has the best house in Texas, and she has a bunch of servants to wait on her, just like a queen. Mom always calls her by her full name—Sara Augusta Patterson Leakey Austin. Mom thinks it makes her sound important. I think Mama Austin probably is really important, so it's extra nice that she lets everyone call her Mama.

Mama Austin is over ninety years old and lives in a town named after her dad. There's a statue of her mom and one of her dad in the center of town. It must be weird to walk past your parents every time you go to the library. Maybe it's good that she's blind now and doesn't have to see the statues of her mom and dad all the time.

We deposit Granddad at Aunt Betty's house and drive like mad to Uvalde, making it in just two days instead of three. My sisters and brothers and I hang out in Big Mama's backyard and don't bother walking to any stores. Dad wins the golf tournament; he takes time to drive us to Mama Austin's house, and then he drives straight back to Uvalde to play golf for one week. I know we are all supposed to miss him, but we can't wait for him to leave so we can run and jump in the Frio River and cool off. My brothers and sisters and I stand along the driveway, with smiles pasted on our faces, and wave to him as he drives away. "Bye, Dad. Bye. Bye, Dad." His car goes faster and faster the farther away from Mama Austin's he gets.

Mama Austin likes everything and everyone; she is the friendliest person I know. She sits in her wheelchair on her front porch all day and smiles. It's hard to know what a blind person has to smile about, but Mama Austin's thin arms and wrinkly skin wave around in front of her when she talks, and she never seems sad that she is blind. Her voice is still strong and loud; when she hollers for her maid, you can hear her clear down by the river. It's too bad that Mama Austin can no longer see the river from her porch. Mama Austin's servants stare at Mike and Danny, but Mama Austin can't see that they are Indian, so she hugs them just like the rest of us.

After Dad leaves, Mom quickly changes into her new black swimming suit and sits on a blanket in the shade of an old live-oak tree. She issues orders to us all. "Danalee, go and get me a Coke and my new *Ellery Queen* book. Marilynn, keep an eye on Mike and Danny and make sure they don't fall in the river. Joellen, keep an eye on D'Nelle and Deanne and make sure they don't kill each other."

Deanne hops up and down on the hot dirt; her bare feet bounce as if she's walking on a bed of hot coals. She knows that Mom is about to disappear into her book and wants an answer before she does. "When can we go swimming?"

Mom opens the book I've handed her and begins to read. She waves her hand in an act of dismissal and says, "Everyone can swim after lunch and naps. Right now, I'm going to sit in the sun and read my book. I suggest you get your own book and do the same."

D'Nelle runs toward the old wooden porch of Mama Austin's and yells over her shoulder, "Mom, I'm going to read to Mama Austin. She likes *Nancy Drew*."

Mama Austin's house is older than she is; she was born here. Giant cypress and pecan trees threaten to push over her ancient wooden house. The Indians burned it down once, but her dad rebuilt it. Morning-glory vines cover the windows and walkways and the porch railings, but who needs to see out of a window when you're blind? Honeysuckle and jasmine vines support the wooden porch beans; without them, the house might crumble. I sit on the porch and drink in the smell of the Mexican food that's being prepared for dinner by Mama Austin's cook.

Texas-sized flies, bees, and grasshoppers hover just off the edge of the porch. Stinging red ants lie in wait for us. A bite from a red ant causes my skin to burn, turn bright red, and itch and itch for days. I know where every anthill is between the house and the river.

After naps, everyone changes into swimming suits and runs for the river. Marilynn yells as she runs past me, carrying Mike, "Hurry up and get your suit on! You have to carry Danny past the anthills."

When Danny and I reach the bank of the river, Mike jumps up and down on the mossy riverbank and yells, "Me in! Me in!" until Marilynn lifts him up and into a shallow pool, where he can stand knee-deep in the cool, motionless water. Danny and I join him in the shallow pool, while everyone else takes turns swinging out over the river by holding on to a knotted rope that is tied to the limb of an old oak tree.

I spend five glorious days swimming; eating tamales; sitting on the porch, reading; and generally, doing nothing. Today, though, everything will change. Dad, Big Mama, J. W., Uncle Bubba, Aunt Grace, and Dad's oldest sister and her kids will arrive this afternoon and stay for supper. Mama Austin doesn't care much for Big Mama, and Big Mama doesn't care much for Mama Austin, but I know they'll try to get along today.

Mama Austin's cook has jobs for each of us, so that she will have supper ready on time. She is an old Mexican woman without any teeth. All week long she's talked to Mike and Danny in Spanish and doesn't understand why they won't answer her. One afternoon, I spend ten minutes trying to explain in my halting Spanish that Mike and Danny are Navajo, not Mexican. I think that she just thinks they are loco.

Marilynn and Joellen shuck corn. D'Nelle cracks pecans for pecan pie. Deanne sits on top of the ice cream maker, and Mike spreads small handfuls of rock salt over the ice while I turn the handle. Danny stands beside Marilynn and tries to pick up the silken hairs from the corn and put them in the paper garbage sack, but the threads of fine hair stick to his hands. He stands and shakes his hands in an attempt to get it off.

Mama Austin's servants dig a big hole in the back yard and line it with sand and charcoal, and then they hang a baby goat on a long stick across the hot coals. All day long, we take turns turning and turning the spit so the goat will cook evenly all the way around.

During Mike's and Danny's naptime, I stand in the bathtub in Mama Austin's tiny bathroom and listen to Marilynn and Joellen argue. I've never seen Joellen so mad. She isn't as tall as Marilynn, but her boobs are as big so in this confined space, when they face each other, one of them has to turn right or left so their boobs won't collide. Red-faced by her anger, Joellen spits when she talks. "You are crazy! When we get home, you tell Philip he's not your boyfriend anymore. Go date Bobby or Billy!"

Marilynn turns a little to the left and says, "I will not! He *is* my boyfriend, and no one can tell us not to like each other."

I know someone who'll tell them a thing or two. I remind them, "Dad will kill both of you. Anyway, you can't have a boyfriend who is the brother of your brother. It's not right."

Marilynn casually says, "We can't help it if my family adopted his baby brother. That doesn't mean I can't like anybody in Danny's family. Philip is really cute."

I can't believe Marilynn is so dumb. Why can't she just date someone else? Every boy in the junior high school wants to date her—she's the prettiest girl in the school. I stand my ground in the cast-iron tub and say, "Does Philip call his brother Danny or Herman? Does his mother know you're his girlfriend? Are you the reason she's been standing outside in the yard, calling for Herman every day?"

Joellen won't turn right or left. Her boobs poke into Marilynn. "You need to get a different boyfriend, or I'm going to tell Mom."

As if on cue, Mom taps on the bathroom door. "What are you going to tell me? Come on, girls. I need you outside. Marilynn, you watch the boys. Your dad will be here any minute, and he's bringing his whole goddamn family with him. Joellen, you and Danalee check on the ice cream. It still needs more turning. Oh, and Joellen, I expect you to tell me what's been going on in there."

The supper is a great success. Big Mama and Mama Austin smile at each other the whole evening. Big Mama doesn't know that Mama Austin smiles at everyone. Uncle Bubba and Aunt Grace smoke cigarettes while they eat. Marilynn, Joellen, and I pick at our food and worry about Mom's finding out that Marilynn's boyfriend is Danny's big brother. Mama Austin's cook runs from table to table and piles more and more food on our plates.

The next day, on our way home to Shiprock, Mom trades places with D'Nelle, and she and Joellen sit in the back of the car and have a quiet conversation. Marilynn sits on the front seat next to Dad, so she can't do anything about it. Mom's head never moves as she listens to Joellen spill her guts. D'Nelle sits in Mom's place and carefully holds Mom's opened bottle of Coca-Cola to her nose and sniffs.

10

Colder Than Cold

When we arrive at Aunt Betty's house, Skeet is happy to see all of us and can't wait to get in the car and leave. My cousins say that Granddad and Aunt Betty had a fight, and she yelled at him to get out, but he didn't have any place to "get to" until we showed up with the car. He sits next to Marilynn and smokes one cigarette after another until we reach Shiprock.

School starts, and I'm pretty sure that Mom hasn't said anything to Dad about Marilynn's boyfriend because Dad is not mad at Marilynn or Mom. He concentrates on preparing his basketball team for this year's round of tournaments. Mom doesn't appear to be mad at Marilynn; she spends most of her time selling Avon to the ladies who live in the Kerr-McGee compound. She likes selling Avon because she gets money for it, but more importantly, she gets free samples of all of the new products. At the moment, she is in love with the scent "Occur." One corner of our living room is crowded with boxes and boxes of Occur perfume and hand lotion. I bet every woman at church who lives in our compound smells like Occur.

When school starts, I don't wait for Bonnie to show up at my house. I run to school each day to try to be the first one to say hi to Mr. Schmidt. My moccasins glide across the familiar dirt path to the school and slide down the linoleum floor of the wide hallway. Mr. Schmidt—always one of the first teachers in the building—can't hear me coming down the hall when I wear my moccasins. I hold the loose ends of my concho belt so that they will not clang together, and I sneak up on him each morning and yell, "Good morning, Mr. Schmidt!"

When the weather turns cold, I can no longer wear my moccasins, and Mr. Schmidt always hears the soles of my tennis shoes squeak on the linoleum. In early December, school is canceled on account of the big game, but I run over to school anyway and say hello to Mr. Schmidt. He and his family will follow Dad's car when everyone in town drives to Window Rock to see the basketball game between the Navajo high school team, called the Thirties, and a visiting team, the Harlem Globetrotters.

We leave early in the afternoon to allow time to reach Window Rock for the evening game. Brother Frank drives the lead pickup truck through the lightly falling snow. On dry pavement, Window Rock is a good four-hour drive; in the snow, it's more like six. Everyone in Shiprock, except the children who live at the boarding school, joins us on the highway. No one wants to miss the big game; the Thirties are undefeated for the season.

Brother Frank drives slower than Dad likes to drive. Exhaust from the car in front of us sneaks into our heater system, so Dad won't turn up the heater full blast. He also worries about the engine overheating because we're driving so slowly, and running the heater all of the time makes the engine hot. He decides to turn off the heater and just run it for ten minutes every thirty minutes. Marilynn is the timekeeper. At this pace, I'm going to freeze before we reach the Civic Center.

Deanne sits on her knees and wiggles her whole body back and forth. "I can't wait, Dad! I'm not kidding. I have to go!"

Dad is not happy. "Shit. Can't you wait until we get there?" Dad concentrates on the snowy road in front of him and sighs. "You'll have to wait until I can find a place to safely pull off the road. When I stop this car, everyone in here better be prepared to make a bathroom stop. I'm not stopping again."

Dad slowly maneuvers our car out of the long line of cars and pulls just far enough off of the road for the cars following us to pass us. Bonnie waves to me as her family's car inches by.

Dad walks around to Granddad's side of the car and yanks open his door. Next, he opens the door beside me. Frigid air rushes into the car. We all frantically button our coats, and Mom yells at Dad, "Are you crazy? Close the goddamn door!"

Dad ignores Mom. He sticks his head into the car and tells Deanne, "Get out here and stand between the doors and go." He looks at the rest of us. "When she's finished, I expect each one of you to do the same." He reaches across my shivering body and lifts Mike and then Danny outside. "Come on, boys, we don't have to hide behind a door."

Granddad laughs from the front seat. "Hey, Joe, why don't you show them injuns how to piss into the wind?"

I have to pee, but I'm too cold to go. Everyone in the car yells at me to hurry up. There's no place to hide in a desert. I worry that everyone in the passing cars can see me squat between the car doors. I don't want to move my feet—urine-soaked ground surrounds me. I close my eyes and think of my secret hideout along the banks of the San Juan River. Soon, warm urine trickles down my legs.

Mom needs to go to the bathroom, too, but she refuses to get out of the car unless Granddad gets out of the front seat and turns his back on the car doors. Granddad isn't getting out of the car and so Mom isn't, either. Dad slams the two car doors and gets back into the car. He rolls down his window and waves his arm up and down until someone lets him pull back into the long line. Instead of a car behind us, we now have a flatbed wagon pulled by two snow-covered horses. Mike and Danny love watching the steam coming out of the horses' noses.

When we reach the Civic Center, Mom bolts from the back of the car and runs to the bathroom. Marilynn holds Mike's hand, and Joellen carries Danny, as we make our way into the Civic Center. Massive timbers cling to the ceiling above us, reminiscent of the interior of a hogan. The Civic Center is used for basketball games during the regular school year, but it has never held this many people before.

Large posters line the walls of the entrance to the Civic Center. Movie posters announce Joel McCrea in *Wichita,* a movie about Wyatt Earp; and Richard Boone and George Hamilton in *A Thunder of Drums,* a movie about cowboys and Indians. According to other posters, Mahalia Jackson performed here last March and Fats Domino last July. I don't know who these people are, but the posters make me wish I'd traveled to Window Rock to see them. In three weeks, Chubby Checker will perform. I'd do dishes for a month if Dad would drive me to Window Rock to see Chubby Checker do the twist.

Wet woolen blankets from the flatbed wagons line the bleachers. The distinct odor of wet wool, combined with an overwhelming amount of cigarette smoke, permeates the interior of the Civic Center. The blue haze of cigarette smoke dominates all available air space. We stand in the entry area and scan the bleachers for Mom, who was supposed to save seats for us after going to the bathroom. She's easy to spot—she's hogging all of the seats near the bottom of the bleachers, next to the radio announcer. Her orange hair has returned to its natural auburn color, brown-framed glasses accent her slender face, and her new penny loafers peek out from under the cuff of her long black pants. She waves her arms in the air when she sees us.

She stuffs our coats and scarves under the bleachers and keeps the box of food and water at her feet. Mike sits to one side of her, his view of the basketball court currently blocked by the backs of people's legs. Danny stands next to her and has a death grip on her collar; he is not used to so many people. Mike and Danny are like night and day when it comes to liking people. Mike is like Mama Austin; he likes everyone. Danny is definitely more like me; for him, alone is better.

Mike continues to be very large for his age. I think it's all the bread that he eats! I call him my baby Buddha. I saw a picture of Buddha in a book in Mrs. Thomas' room, and Mike looks just like him. Danny likes people but in small doses. Someone has to be willing to sit beside him for a long time and just talk quietly to him before he'll ever smile. Now that Deanne is getting older and doesn't need Lady to protect her, Lady has taken to following Danny around.

The radio announcer who sits next to us turns on the microphone and says, "Welcome! Welcome to Window Rock's beautiful Civic Center. Hurry and take your seats. The game is about to begin."

I search the stands for Bonnie. The families from Shiprock are scattered all over the gymnasium. D'Nelle, Deanne and I sit on the bleacher seats directly behind Mom. I save a seat for Bonnie, but I'm not sure I'll see her in this mass of people. Marilynn and Joellen climb to the top of the bleachers and sit with some high school kids from Shiprock. Once she's out of Dad's sight, Marilynn takes off the old gray sweatshirt she's had on all day and sticks out her chest in her new tight red sweater. Joellen has a chest, but she's afraid to show it to anybody, so she never takes off her green corduroy coat.

Dad and Granddad sit on the bleacher seats next to Mike. Mike rests his hand on Dad's leg whenever someone tries to talk to him. Dad and Granddad puff their cigarettes in unison and ignore the rest of us. Dad's body is so erect, he looks like you could saw him in half. He's jealous that he's not the coach of the Thirties basketball team. Granddad's taller than anybody in the room. He refused Mom's plea to wear his teeth to the game, and much to Mom's dismay, he opens a metal tin of sardines right before the game starts and dumps them onto a slice of bread for his evening meal.

Several white women stop to ask Mom where she found the little Navajo boys, as if we could just go to the grocery store and pick up two Navajo brothers. I've grown used to people asking about Mike and Danny. I didn't know it was so popular to adopt Navajo boys. Mom is tired of people asking her about Mike and Danny, and now, instead of being polite, she tells the person to go talk to the judge in Window Rock.

I give up trying to find Bonnie or anyone else from Shiprock, and so I watch the radio announcer. He takes a puff on his cigarette and then talks into the microphone with his mouth full of smoke. I can't wait to see the Globetrotters. Dad and Granddad have argued all week about who's going to win the game.

Granddad says that injuns are better basketball players than niggers, so he's betting on the Thirties.

Dad shrugs his shoulders and says nobody's beaten the Globetrotters, and although he's never seen them play, he's betting on someone named Meadowlark Lemon to win the game. I think I have a weird name, but I can't imagine being named after a bird.

Whistles hang around the necks of the referees, and rule books stick out of their back pockets. The high school boys, the Thirties, take the floor, followed by the Globetrotters. My eyes nearly pop out of my head when I get a look at the Harlem Globetrotters. I knew the Globetrotters were Negro, but I didn't know they were giants!

The radio announcer says, "This is it, folks. The ref is holding the ball for the toss-up. The ball is in the air and … it's a Globetrotter ball. Oh, my gosh, folks, faster than I can blink, the Globetrotters make the first basket. It's two for the Globetrotters and zero for the Thirties."

Dad grumbles, "Goddamn lead feet."

The announcer is so excited, he can hardly stay in his seat. "Young Bobby of the Thirties inbounds the ball. The Thirties dribble and pass their way up court. These Globetrotters are giants, folks, just giants! Stuart has the ball; he's going in for a layup, and it's now two to two. The Thirties have tied the score!

"Folks, the Globetrotter's have the ball—wait … the referee is signaling for the Globetrotter to hand the ball to him. Meadowlark will not give the ball to the ref. This is unbelievable, folks. Meadowlark has one hand on the ref's head and with the other hand, he's pretending to give the ball to the ref. The ref is trying, folks. He's trying to grab the ball, but he just can't reach it."

This guy who won't give the basketball to the ref is the guy who Dad thinks is going to win the game for the Globetrotters. Every time the ref reaches for the ball, the members of the Globetrotters laugh, but no one in the Civic Center is laughing.

"What the hell?" Granddad says.

I wonder if Meadowlark Lemon has noticed that none of the Navajo in the audience will look at him. The Navajo consider it rude to stare at someone, and Meadowlark seems to delight in running up to the bleachers and staring into the audience. I wonder if someone should tell him not to be so rude.

Meadowlark finally hands the ball to the ref, and the game proceeds but not for long. I think the radio announcer is going to have a conniption fit. "Meadowlark inbounds the ball and—wait … wait … folks, I wish you could see this. The ball is sailing in the air from the half-court line and wait … my gosh … oh my gosh! Unbelievable, folks! J. C. Gipson makes the basket from the half-court line! Stupendous!"

Dad shakes his head from side to side. The shaken high school team member prepares to inbound the ball, but every Globetrotter on the court jumps up and down in front of him. The refs blow their whistles and yell at the Globetrotters to return to their proper positions. I've never seen a team behave this way. They must be undefeated, because they scare the other team to death.

Stuart, a member of the Thirties, inbounds the ball. The Thirties make a basket, and when the Globetrotters inbound the ball, Meadowlark catches it and starts dribbling—under his legs, behind his back, two inches off the floor—and spins around while he dribbles; it is magnificent. The high school boys don't know what to do except stand and admire him. When Meadowlark finishes his dribbling show, the game resumes, but I think the Thirties team members would rather watch Meadowlark dribble than play basketball.

The radio announcer sits still in his chair for a change and announces, "A Globetrotter inbounds the ball to the ref, instead of to one of his own players! This is unbelievable! What kind of a ball is this? Folks, the ball is not bouncing; it just wobbles around on the floor. Every time the ref tries to pick up the ball, Meadowlark pushes it with his toe, and it takes off across the floor. Our boys don't know what to make of this, although it is funny. That poor ref—he just can't catch up with the ball. I can't help but laugh, and it looks like our team has been infected with the laughter bug as well!"

I laugh. Dad and Granddad laugh and both say "Well, shit" at the same time. Mike claps his hands and laughs. It finally dawns on the audience that Meadowlark and his teammates are here to be silly, not to play a real game of basketball. When the game is over, I don't want to go home. Dad gathers up the box of food and remaining water and heads to the car. He hollers over his shoulder to us, "I want every one of you girls to go to the bathroom before you get in the car!"

After we've gone to the bathroom, we huddle by the front door and wait for Dad's signal that the car is warmed up and the snow cleared from the windows. While we were sitting in the Civic Center and laughing, it looks like it snowed about twelve or fourteen inches—the cars and flatbed wagons are buried in snow. The Navajo who own the flatbed wagons decide to leave their horses in a makeshift barn and spend the night in the Civic Center. I think that makes a lot of sense, and I think we should spend the night with them. When Dad signals us to run to the car, frigid air fills my lungs and nose. Snow streams down like a thundershower. I beat everyone to the car and scramble to the far back.

Dad drives very, very slowly. Brother Frank's pickup truck continually gets stuck in the snow, and Dad and several men from the other cars get out to help him get unstuck. Dad's hands turn blue, and the fourth time the truck gets stuck, he can't help because he can't feel his fingers. Mom makes him stick his hands under the heater vent and keep them there, while we wait for the others to help Brother Frank.

I have never been so cold in my life. I take short tiny breaths, just enough to get some air in my lungs. My lips turn purple. Danny tries to climb inside Mom's coat and eventually, she unzips it and lets him in. I can tell she is scared and her fear makes me scared, too. She tries to whisper to Dad but we all hear her. "Joe, I'm really frightened. The kids are getting pretty cold. Can't we go any faster?"

Dad's light blue hands grip the steering wheel. "Hon, we're going as fast as we can. It's better that Brother Frank's big old pickup plows through the snow first; it makes it easier for our car to stay on the road. Have everyone snuggle together in the middle; their body warmth will help keep them warm. Not you, Danalee—you're sitting in the back, and I need your help. The headlights from the car behind us make it hard for me to see the road in front of us. I need you to sit up straight and block his lights. Jo, give her a blanket, and the rest of you—snuggle."

Mom and Marilynn gather my siblings between them. Danny lies with his back against Mom's chest and Mike crawls in next to Marilynn. Joellen completes the circle of Mom and Marilynn, and D'Nelle and Deanne climb into the middle. I spread the blankets across Mom, Marilynn, and Joellen's backs; they look like a large patchwork quilt. D'Nelle and Deanne have the coats piled high on them. I can no longer see Mike and Danny. I pull the blanket Joellen gave me tightly around my back and sit with my back to the rear window. I hug my knees to my chest and wrap the other end of the blanket around my legs. Joellen pokes her head out from under her blanket. She looks serious when she whispers, "Don't freeze to death."

When my head begins to droop and I briefly fall asleep, Dad yells from the front seat, "Danalee, wake up! I'm sorry, hon, but I need you to sit up straight."

I stare at the huddle of sleeping bodies in front of me. I watch Marilynn's chin drop to her chest and then jerk straight up in her attempt to stay awake. I wonder what to think about that might help me stay awake. I try to remember each play of the basketball game. I pretend that Meadowlark Lemon picks me out of the crowd of people to make the game's winning shot. The radio announcer tells the world:

"World-famous Harlem Globetrotter Meadowlark Lemon thrills the amazed audience with his magical dribbling. He stops the game to shake hands with a little white girl, who is sitting in the bleachers, and shows her how to dribble the basketball under her leg and behind her back. Soon, she is as good as Meadowlark. She tosses the ball in the basket from the right. She tosses it in from the left. She turns on a dime and sinks one from half-court. The crowd of friends and family are amazed at her skill. She becomes the first ten-year-old white girl to play center for the world-famous Harlem Globetrotters. Meadowlark tells the little white girl—"

"Goddamn it, Danalee! Sit the fuck up! Those lights are blinding me!" Dad's voice rings out in the car. I'm not a world-famous basketball player. I'm a freezing little girl who needs to go to the bathroom.

Having to go to the bathroom keeps me awake and helps me to sit up straight for the next hundred miles. When we reach home, Dad doesn't let any of us go into the house until he figures out why the lights are out. Almost as soon as he enters the house, he comes back to the car carrying Lady, all wrapped up in a blanket. He lays Lady on the backseat and tells Deanne to lie down beside her and give her lots of hugs. Mom's eyes silently ask Dad if Lady is dead. Dad shakes his head. "The heat's off in the house, and Lady's pretty cold. I think she'll be fine, but she needs some help to warm up."

Dad has stuffed his hurting hands inside his coat pocket. "Now, this is what we are going to do. Mom and Skeet are going to come into the house with me, and we're going to get Danalee and Joellen's bed ready for all of you. You'll be much warmer all huddled into the same bed than alone. When I signal, I want you all to go straight to the bathroom and then to Danalee's bed, and get under the covers—that means Lady, too. I don't want you to flush the toilet; just go and then run get under the covers. Mom and I will get our bed ready with extra blankets, and then we'll come to get Mike and Danny, and they'll sleep with us. Marilynn, bring all of the blankets from the car inside. Skeet and Mom and I will need them. Now, does everyone understand what I want you to do? In the morning, just stay under the covers until I tell you it's okay to come out. Skeet and I will try to figure out the propane tank in the morning, when it's light. If you have to go to the bathroom, I want you to go fast and get back under the covers. Go ahead and leave on all your clothes—no pj's tonight."

When Dad tells us it's okay to come inside, I'm the first one in the bathroom and the first one in bed. I'll be happy if everyone piles on top of me. The air in the bedroom is so cold, it hurts my nose and mouth to breathe in. Lady and my sisters pile up on top of me, and we try to sleep. I'm worried about Granddad. If it's better for all of us to snuggle and not sleep alone, who is snuggling with Granddad to help keep him warm?

In the morning we stay in bed until Dad and Granddad fix the propane heater, but we keep the thermometer on a low setting because Dad doesn't know when the propane tank man will be able to make it through the snow to refill the tank. The snow is so deep that no one is driving their cars or trucks on the roads.

We spend three days in the bed, under the covers. We eat cereal for breakfast, lunch, and supper until we run out of milk. Mom wears her coat and four pair of socks and stands in the kitchen and cooks oatmeal, until we run out of oatmeal. We eat all of the spaghetti by the fourth day. The day after we got home, Dad walked to the trading post to buy a few things, but Jim wasn't selling anything to the people who live in Shiprock. During really bad winter storms, Jim loads his flatbed wagon with food and water and heads out to help the Navajo families trapped by the storm. The Navajo families who live outside of Shiprock don't have electricity for lights or propane tanks for heat. If the snow buries their sheep, they don't have sheep's milk to drink or sheep to eat; Jim says they can starve to death.

Each day, Granddad listens to the radio to see when the storm will stop. We learn that on the day of the big game it snowed fourteen inches in Window Rock—no wonder we had trouble driving home. Today's announcement lets us know that the storm might be worse than we can see from Shiprock. The President has declared the Navajo reservation a disaster area; the temperature was -25 degrees in Farmington yesterday. I feel sorry for all of the kids who live at the boarding school who can't go home. They have to stay in the boarding school and worry about what has happened to their moms and dads and brothers and sisters.

The man on the radio says that pilots from Kelly Air Force base will fly C-47 transports and C-119 cargo planes and make emergency food and hay drops on the reservation. Stranded sheep, goats, dogs, and horses will receive over 1,300 bales of hay. They will also drop food packages for stranded Navajo families that include flour, sugar, coffee, potatoes, and shortening. It's called Operation Hay Lift, and it feels a little like Christmas. Yesterday, we ate all of Granddad's remaining cans of sardines for supper. Today, we are down to the last jar of peanut butter.

Finally, the storm breaks, the temperatures rise, and the snow begins to melt. Dad and most of the other men who live in Shiprock begin to clear the highway of snow. On the day the road to Farmington is cleared, a long line of cars streams to the grocery store in Farmington, just like the long line of cars that traveled to the Civic Center. I am consumed by thoughts of starving to death.

11

Canada

Something's wrong with Granddad. Nobody wants to talk about it, but I can tell. The sadness he felt when Grandma died has never gone away, only now he is sometimes sad and mean. Well, not mean, as if he'll hit you; it's more the cruel kind of mean, especially toward Mom. He says things to her that he knows will make her cry, and he does it on purpose. He didn't used to be like that. When Grandma was alive, Granddad laughed and made jokes. The only jokes he makes now are meant to hurt someone's feelings. I feel sorry for Mike and Danny—he never says one word to them. I think Mom wishes he'd never say one word to her.

I think I'm Granddad's only friend in the world. He lets me sit next to him and listen to the radio with him. I take him a glass of water when his coughing gets really bad. Marilynn says she hopes he coughs himself to death, but I know she doesn't really mean that. Marilynn is just mad all the time these days and, like Granddad, she blames everyone. She really only has herself to blame. She's in Dad's school now, and when she won all of the races in the March track-and-field meet, Dad told her she had hidden talent for a fourteen-year-old. He's going to help her find her talent, and Marilynn's really mad about that. Dad thinks that anyone with athletic talent should play golf so he's going to teach Marilynn how to play golf. Marilynn would rather use her talent to wear short-shorts and wear a tight shirt and run track in front of the junior high boys.

I sit on the porch of the abandoned schoolhouse and wait for Dad and Marilynn to show up for the lesson. Joellen grabs my arm and pulls me back against the wooden wall of the old porch. "Sh-h! Be quiet!" she whispers. "If he sees us, we're going to have to do it, too."

Joellen is still shorter than I am, but she's strong, and when she pulls my arm or gives me a shove, I feel like I'll be bruised for a week. I'm still so skinny that any shove does leave me with a big blue bruise. Taking out my tonsils didn't do a thing for my weight. Joellen and I slowly peek around the corner of the porch to stare at Marilynn. She stands in the bright late-morning sunlight and tightens the red rubber band that secures her ponytail. She is tall for a fourteen-year-old and incredibly pretty. She has on her new white tennis shoes with clean, white, unmarred shoelaces. Dad tells her that her cleatless shoes are okay for lessons, but she'll have to buy real golf shoes when she plays golf with Dad.

She stands to the side and watches as Dad meticulously ties the laces on his favorite red and white golf shoes. The brief morning rain shower has settled the desert dust so that the cleats of his shoes leave tiny holes in the dirt as he walks over to his golf bag. He lifts different clubs in and out of the bag, inspecting the head of each club for any sign of dirt. He selects a nine iron for Marilynn's first lesson. He then turns and gives her his full attention.

Marilynn briefly glances over Dad's shoulder and sees us spying on her. She then focuses on the lightweight nine iron in her hands, and for the first time in a long time, she listens to what Dad has to say. Holding a seven iron, Dad demonstrates the proper grip.

"Put the handle in your left hand, with your thumb on top of the handle. Take the index finger of your left hand, and put it between the little finger and ring finger of your right hand, like this."

Marilynn mimics Dad's moves. Joellen and I strain to see around Dad's back so that we can see the secret handgrip.

Dad stares at his own hands and continues the lesson. "Take your right hand and wrap it around the club handle, with your palm on top of your left thumb. Let's see. Good.

"Now place the head of the club on the ground in front of you, bend your knees a little, bend your head down, and keep your eyes on the ball. When you swing, you're going to pull the club straight back to here, then turn your shoulders and pull the club up toward your left shoulder. Then in one motion, shift your weight to your left leg, pull down and through with your left arm, and hit the ball in the middle of the club head. Then, turn your shoulders and let the club go all the way back to your right shoulder. Remember to keep your head down and your eyes on the ball at all times."

Marilynn concentrates and listens to every word he says. With her feet planted shoulder width apart, head down, knees slightly bent, the thumb of her left hand covered by the palm of her right, and most importantly, her eyes on the ball, she nods her head as if she understands every one of Dad's directions. Joellen and I smile to ourselves; we're proud of Marilynn. We know she's really going to whack that little white ball.

She pulls the club slowly back, just like Dad said to do, and turns her shoulders and upper body as the club lifts into the air behind her right shoulder. She shifts her weight to her left side, pulls the club down toward the waiting white sphere, closes her eyes, and swings.

Her club barely reaches the full height of the back swing before Dad starts in. "I told you to keep your fucking eyes open! You're not going to hit a fucking thing with your eyes closed."

Marilynn stares at the traitorous white ball. She quietly mumbles, "Okay, Dad."

Joellen and I stare, too. We're shocked that Marilynn missed the ball. Marilynn is good at everything—roller-skating, baton twirling, hula hooping—so we can't believe this.

Dad calms down and talks to Marilynn as if she were a six-year-old. "Now try it again, and this time keep your head down and your eyes on the ball."

Marilynn gives Dad a weak smile and then places the head of the club next to the ball. Feet apart, hands in the secret grip, head down, and eyes on the ball, she swings again. The nine iron hits the top of the ball, and it rolls about three feet before slowing to a stop.

Marilynn stares at the ball and practices the secret grip, while Dad paces back and forth in front of her, cigarette smoke swirling around his head. He tries to keep his voice calm. "Goddamn it, Marilynn. You've got to keep your head down and your eyes on the ball in order to hit it. Try it again."

Marilynn bends her knees and wiggles her butt and takes a practice swing. She says with more confidence, "Okay, Dad." She takes a deep breath and tries it again ... and again ... and again. Every time that Dad says "fuck" or "goddamn it," Marilynn just says, "Okay, Dad." Joellen and I know that Marilynn is determined not to let Dad make her cry. We see tears form in the bottom half of her eyes, and her lower lip begins to tremble, but she does not cry.

Joellen boldly leaves her hiding place so that Marilynn can see her. She bends her knees and swings her butt and pretends to hold a golf club in front of her in preparation for her swing. I stomp softly back and forth in front of Joellen, puff my invisible cigarette, and pretend to yell. Marilynn's eyes flicker from Joellen to Dad, as she now tries not to laugh. Exasperated, Dad grabs the nine iron from her hands and slams it into the golf bag. Marilynn, Joellen, and I bite the insides of our cheeks in an attempt not to laugh out loud. He tosses the bag onto his right shoulder and stomps away. The only remnants of Marilynn's golf lesson are the tiny cleat holes that Dad leaves in the dirt.

Two days later, we're sure that everyone in the compound can hear Dad as he stands at the front door and yells at the top of his lungs, "Marilynn! Get in here!"

He smokes a cigarette and paces up and down in the living room. Granddad sits at the dining room table with a smile on his face. Mom holds open the screen door and waits for Marilynn to come in from the yard. D'Nelle is now old enough to understand when it's best to just leave the room; she herds Mike, Danny, and a protesting Deanne down the hallway to her room. Joellen and I sit at the kitchen table, our hearts pounding.

Marilynn stands in front of Dad while he grills her. "What's the matter with you? This afternoon, Mr. Riley asked me to tell you to stop meeting Philip after school. Philip gets a ride home, and when he misses his ride, he has a five-mile walk out to the hogan. Mr. Riley knows that Mary needs him at home to help with the kids and tend to the sheep. I know you are not a complete idiot; you *do* know who Philip is." Dad resumes pacing as he thinks of something else to say. Marilynn just stares at the floor and waits. Dad stops in front of her and continues, his voice a little less angry. "What kind of an example are you setting for your sisters? What's your plan for the future? Are you going to marry a Navajo and move into a hogan and learn how to raise sheep? You will stop this relationship right now. I know you are old enough to date, but you are going to date a white boy."

Dad stares at Marilynn; Marilynn stares at Dad and then past him to Mom. I see her chest rise and fall with each deep breath. I'm sure that Marilynn isn't going to marry Philip and learn to raise sheep; he is just a boyfriend. I wait for her to speak up, but while I wait, I hear Mary doing her daily cry for Herman.

Everyone in the living room shifts their attention to the front door. Dad looks around the room. "Danalee! Get outside and tell Mary to go home. I'm tired of this shit!"

For weeks, Mary has come to our house every day, wanting to see Herman. Today, she stands by the picket fence and searches the empty yard. "Herman," she cries. "Herman!"

I slowly walk toward Mary and wonder what to say to her. Except for her flat belly, she looks the same as she did two years ago when I first saw her. I know she's walked five miles to see Danny. I know she wants Danny back; she is sorry she let us adopt him. I try to understand her point of view, but Danny is my brother. I don't think she should get to take him back. I don't speak Navajo, and I don't know sign language. I hear Dad lecturing Marilynn again, and I'm glad Mary doesn't speak English.

"There are plenty of white boys at school," I hear Dad say. "You can date one of them. If your grades don't improve you won't be dating anybody. No roller-skating! No basketball games! No listening to records at Lucy's house."

Mary is going to make me miss everything that happens in the living room. I want her to just go home and be happy with her other six children. When she sees me, Mary turns to me and says, "Herman?"

I shake my head from side to side. "No, Herman. Go home. Go." I wave my arms toward the cattle guard, hoping she will get the message. She stares at the yard as if Herman might magically appear, but she finally turns and walks away. I watch her leave. She looks so sad; I decide that it must be horrible to watch your son grow up with another family and not be able to talk to him. I wonder if Mom and Dad will let Mary come to visit when Danny is older. I wonder if Danny would like to meet all of his Navajo brothers and sisters.

I return to my position in the kitchen and feel sorry for Mary and for Marilynn. Dad and Granddad join forces against Marilynn. Granddad slaps the top of the dining room table and asks Marilynn, "You want to be a goddamn squaw? You want to have a bunch of little half-breeds running around here? You—"

Mom walks up to Marilynn and puts her arm around her shoulders. "All right. That's enough. Marilynn, go to your room."

It's clear to Joellen and me that Mom has kept Marilynn's secret from last summer. She probably kept Marilynn's secret to prevent a scene like this one. Joellen and I follow Marilynn down the hallway to our room. Joellen could say "I told you so," but Marilynn's had enough people yelling at her for one day.

Marilynn and Philip break up. Within a day, Marilynn has four different invitations to go to the new drive-in movie theater, but she is grounded. She has to be in the house each day within ten minutes of the end of school. Dad questions her each evening about her daily activities—who she spoke with and who she had lunch with. Mom gives her extra chores to do so that Marilynn has little time for anything else.

After supper, Mom and Dad go for long walks along the highway. When they return I can always tell they've been talking about something serious. I wonder if they are thinking of some horrible punishment for Marilynn for having a Navajo boyfriend. I have trouble understanding why Marilynn is being punished at all. Will Mike and Danny be punished if they bring home a white girlfriend? What's wrong with having a Navajo boyfriend? I have lots of Navajo friends. Maybe one day I'll have a Navajo boyfriend.

Late one night, I discover what Mom and Dad have been talking about on their long walks. I hear muffled voices and leave my warm bed to sneak down the hallway to the door of the kitchen. Mom, Dad, and Granddad huddle around the small kitchen table. The dim light from the kitchen's overhead fixture spills onto the floor, and I watch cockroaches scramble for cover. I sit with my back to the hallway wall and hug my legs to my chest.

Dad's angry voice whispers, "We got the letter from the Australian Consulate today. They say that they don't let Indians into their fucking country, so I didn't get the coaching job in Sydney."

Granddad's gruff voice offers, "Goddamn smart of them."

Mom whispers, "Well, Joe, I guess you should take the job at the high school in Maricopa."

Dad sounds unhappy about that job. "Another fucking town in a desert … but I *have* been thinking about that job. Phoenix is only thirty miles from Maricopa. You could drive into Phoenix and go to college at Arizona State University and get your teaching certificate. Then we'd both have summers off."

Mom's shocked voice matches my surprise. "You think I could become a teacher?"

I hear the match strike as Dad lights up a cigarette. "Yeah. You're always telling us how smart you are. Now you can show us. You'll make more money being a teacher than being a fucking Avon lady, and God knows we need the money."

Granddad's voice rises above a whisper. "I ain't babysitting no goddamn injuns while Jo Eva goes off to college. She can stay home like her mother did and take care of all of these kids that she keeps bringing home."

Dad raises his voice to the same level as Granddad's. "I'm not asking you to babysit. I'm not an idiot. She can go to school at night, after Marilynn gets home from school, and she can take classes on the weekends. Why don't you write to them, Jo and get an application? You can start in September."

Mom's voice is full of excitement. "I could start this summer if we move right after school is over. We can drive to Phoenix in one day."

Dad tempers Mom's excitement. "Well, I have other plans for us for the summer. You'll have to start in September."

I close my eyes and pray to Grandma:

Dear Grandma,

I don't want to leave Shiprock. What will happen if we end up in a town that's like Uvalde, where Mike and Danny can't go into a store?

Mom seems surprised by Dad's announcement. "What plans? You haven't said anything to me about summer plans."

Dad sounds all apologetic and mushy. "We have two months before we have to be in Maricopa for the start of school. My coaching contract doesn't say anything about showing up early, so why should we? I think we should take a little trip."

Granddad's guarded voice points out, "Two months isn't a little trip. You expect me to stay with Betty for two months while you play golf in Uvalde? No, thank you."

Dad's voice is filled with his own excitement. "I wasn't thinking of going to Texas this summer. I thought we'd head up to Seattle and see some of the World's Fair, and I'd play a little golf. Then we'd drive on up to Canada and see the Canadian Rockies, and I'd play a little golf. We can cross the border at Montana and see Glacier National Park, and I'd play a little golf, and then we'd drive down to Arizona and get settled in Maricopa before school starts. The high school's principal has found us a house to rent, so we don't have to worry about that. What do you think?"

Mom is stunned. "The Seattle World's Fair? Elvis is filming a movie there! Maybe we'll see him."

Dad is pleased that Mom likes his idea. "It's time for a new car so I thought we'd get one of those new Ford Falcon station wagons—it ought to hold all of us. We can get a roof rack for the top of the car and pack the tent and camping gear up there. If we stay at campgrounds, it won't be too expensive. Your dad and the kids can sleep in the tent, and you and I can sleep in the back of the car."

Granddad's voice jumps in. "Like hell! You can sleep in the tent, and I'll sleep in the car, and you can keep that goddamn dog with you, too."

I crawl down the hallway and climb into my bed. We are leaving Shiprock. I can't believe it. In a few weeks, I'll be stuck in the backseat of a new car with Lady, and when I come home from Canada I'll pack up and move to someplace called Maricopa. I hate the idea. What is Dad thinking? I keep Dad's bright idea to myself—no use making everyone miserable.

Granddad suddenly stops being miserable and goes on a cleaning and fixing spree. A few days following the kitchen meeting, I find him in the space between the duplex and the mobile home. An old blanket lies on the ground with the components of his car's engine spread out before him.

I try to turn around and sneak away before he hears me, but I'm too late. Granddad's loud voice bounces off the engine's guts. "I hear you, little shit. If you touch one thing on this blanket, I'll break both your hands."

Granddad doesn't scare me. I sit next to him. "What are you doing to your car?"

He picks up a small round piece of metal and sprays it gold. "I saw you in the hallway the other night. I know that you know we're moving. I think we might want to make a good impression on our new neighbors in Maricopa."

I don't know what he means. "We make a good impression. There's nothing wrong with us."

Granddad explains, "With a couple of dirty injuns living with us, you're going to have to learn to be careful when we leave Shiprock. Not everyone thinks injuns are nice to have around. Just because your daddy tells those two that they're white doesn't mean they are. They'll learn to hate soon enough, and so will you."

Granddad is probably right. I don't want to leave Shiprock. I don't want to live where people are afraid of Mike and Danny because they are Indian. I stare at the golden engine pieces and wonder how this will impress anyone. Who's going to see under the hood of the car?

Granddad can't wait to leave Shiprock. He pats my arm and says, "There's no future for any of you here. For once in his life, your father's being smart, even if you don't like it. Stop sulking. Let's go in and have a sardine sandwich while the paint dries. I'll tell you about the time I first saw your Grandma."

I don't understand what's smart about leaving Shiprock or why this is the first smart thing Dad's ever done. Besides, Grandma's told me a hundred times about the time she first met Granddad.

Sitting at the kitchen table, I smile at Granddad and chew and chew, hoping he'll turn away so I can spit the wad of sardine and bread into my napkin. I don't really like sardine sandwiches, but how Granddad met Grandma is my favorite story. I used to beg Grandma to tell me about the time she rode her horse over to meet Granddad. She'd always pretend like she'd told it too many times, but then she'd take a long, slow drag on her cigarette and start the story.

Granddad swallows his sardine sandwich almost whole, drains his coffee cup, takes a long drag on his cigarette, and then starts talking. His voice is soft and far away, and I look away, embarrassed to intrude on his memories of Grandma.

His voice quivers a little as he says, "Your grandma was the prettiest goddamn woman in Texas. She and her cousin Jimmy Lou used to sneak into the movie house that my pa owned and pretend to watch the movie. I knew she was really there to listen to my music. She always liked it when I played the piano for the movies.

"The day that I rode out to meet her on the ranch was bitter cold. It felt like it might rain or snow or both. She had an old brown horse named Bess that wasn't much bigger than she was. She loved that goddamn horse. I stood by the bank of the river and watched them coming. Your Grandma was pushing ol' Bess as if a bear was chasing her. Her hair flew straight back, like Bess' tail. She had on a white blouse that filled with the cold air as she rode. Your crazy grandma didn't have on a hat or a coat. She and Bess stopped about two feet in front of me.

"I was worried that Bess might collapse, she was breathing so hard, but your grandma just sat in the saddle and stared down at me—didn't even get off of her horse. I couldn't move. She was so beautiful. She wasn't a city girl, with rouge and jewelry and fancy clothes. I wanted to marry her right then and there, but we had to wait for the next month. Her pa hated me. My pa hated her. We didn't care. I don't think there was anybody that could have prevented us from getting married."

Granddad stops talking. Tears slide down his caved-in cheeks and across his toothless mouth. His lips fall inward, where teeth used to be. I wish I hadn't asked him to talk about Grandma. I wish I knew how to make him stop missing her so much. Granddad mumbles through his tears, "Goddamn it, Doris. You weren't supposed to die."

The day to leave for Canada arrives. My sisters are still in shock from the news of Dad's plan. Like me, Marilynn and Joellen can't imagine leaving Shiprock. D'Nelle is interested in the World's Fair and can't wait to get to Seattle. Deanne and Lady don't care where we go, as long and they can sit next to each other in the car. Mike's and Danny's lives revolve around how much food they can eat in a day; Mike can still eat twice as much as Danny ever will.

The furniture in our tiny duplex is covered with sheets. Our clothes are packed, and the suitcases ready for Dad to load. The schoolteachers compound is quiet; families have already taken off for the summer. We're the last family to leave. Bonnie's parents stand next to the car, talking to Mom and Dad. They're going to take care of the house while we are gone for two months.

I know it's time to leave, but I can't, not now.

Joellen taps on the bathroom door for the third time. "Come on, Danalee, hurry up. I need to go, too. Granddad's in the other one, and he's going to take forever."

I crack the bathroom door to see who else is in the hallway. "Joellen, I'm bleeding. What should I do?"

Joellen's getting to be like Marilynn; she knows everything. I know I've started my period, but I don't know what to do now. I do know that I don't want Dad to know. Last month, when Joellen didn't go to the baseball game with us, he announced to his team, "She has *the disease* and has the cramps." Joellen died from embarrassment when she heard about his comments. I don't want Dad to announce to Bonnie's parents that I have *the disease*.

Joellen shows me the intricacies of how to use a sanitary napkin and belt and helps me hide some extra napkins in the pockets of my shorts. When Joellen started her period, Mom said, "I thought Marilynn started early, and now you. I guess all of you girls are just lucky."

Lucky? I don't feel lucky. I'm just eleven and a half years old. I don't want to have a period. Joellen is going to tell Dad that she needs to go to the bathroom when it's time for me to change my pad; then Dad won't suspect anything. Joellen is my best friend.

When I make my way outside, Dad stands by the side of the car and yells at Deanne. "Get in the car, or I'll leave you and the goddamn dog behind!" Lady runs around the elementary school playground just one more time. We all know that Dad will not drive off and leave Lady behind, much less Deanne, although some of us think that wouldn't be a bad idea.

Lady and Deanne scurry into the back of the car, settle into a corner, and munch on some of Lady's dog biscuits. Now they both stink. Mom sits cross-legged behind the driver's seat and counts her bottles of Coca-Cola in the tiny ice chest beside her. Mike sits beside her, tearing the middle out of a slice of white bread and rolling it into a ball.

Danny sits in Joellen's lap and listens to her recitation of *How Butterflies Fly*, the forgotten bookmobile book that is now on its way to Canada. D'Nelle hunches over by the car's rear window and consumes a *Nancy Drew* mystery. Every now and then, she turns around and tells Deanne to "stop crunching." Deanne has grown into a giant pest; she loves to bug everyone. Sometimes I think she's mad because she's not the baby of the family anymore, so she keeps acting like one until we all notice her.

Granddad sits in his assigned seat and slowly rolls a cigarette and lights up. Dad pulls a cigarette from the squished package in his shirt pocket and lights up. Marilynn, sitting between them, looks through the blur of smoke at the small group of Navajo boys and girls who've gathered in front of the junior high school across the street to say good-bye. Silent, unnoticed tears run down her face.

Sitting behind Granddad's seat, I lean my head against the car window and try to figure out how to sit comfortably while wearing a long, thick sanitary napkin. I watch Bonnie and her parents walk across the cattle guard and head to their home. I don't think Bonnie will ever have to leave Shiprock. I wonder if Bonnie's family could adopt me.

The thirty bananas that Mom insists on taking with us smell like dirty socks. We're supposed to eat one banana a day. The odor, mixed with tobacco and stale Avon perfume, creates toxic fumes. I roll my window down farther and breathe in the dust of Shiprock. Mom holds her bottle of Coca-Cola close to her nose and breathes in the familiar scent.

Dad drives north into Utah, then Idaho, part of Oregon, and finally into Seattle. It takes a week of our two months to reach Seattle. I'm already tired of sleeping in a tent with Lady and Mom and Dad. The only thing that keeps me going is the thought of going to the Seattle World's Fair. Mr. Schmidt told me before I left that John Glenn's spacecraft, *Friendship 7*, is going to be at the Fair; that's the first thing I want to see.

The walk from the parking lot to the ticket counter takes thirty minutes. I can't believe Granddad is going to the Fair. He even put on a clean shirt for the occasion. He's the only one who's gotten any sleep for the past five days. We wait in the shade of a massive tree while Dad and Mom buy tickets to the Fair. I watch as they stand at the ticket window and argue. Dad shakes his head no, over and over. Mom grabs his arm when he turns to walk away without buying tickets, and he just jerks his arm away and walks toward us. I know what he'll say before he reaches us.

It costs too much. We can't afford to take ten people to the Fair. He suggests that we walk around a bit and then head out to the golf course. We see the monorail speed by. The top of the Space Needle looks like a flying saucer. Mom rushes over to a crowd of people that she hopes are watching Elvis make his movie, but the crowd of people is just in line to buy corn dogs. We return to the car and let Lady run around and go to the bathroom and then silently, we pile back into the car.

On the way to the freeway we see the movie set where Elvis is filming, but it's lunchtime and the only people there are security guards. As we have for the past five days, we wait in the parking lot of the golf course while Dad plays nine holes. Today, Mom and Granddad spread the map across the hood of the car and plot their own vacation.

After Dad's golf game, Mom holds the worn map in her hands and approaches Dad while he stuffs his bag of clubs into the carrier on top of the car. She says in a bright, cherry voice, "Joe, I'd like to stop before we reach Vancouver. There's a campground right before we cross the border into Canada. The kids can get a look at the Pacific Ocean, and we can drive into Vancouver in the morning for your game."

Wow! Mom sounds just like Grandma. Dad pauses for a second and then agrees. Once Mom starts asking for things, the trip gets a lot better. In Vancouver, she makes Dad drop us off at Stanley Park, and we wait for him there, rather than in the parking lot of the golf course. On the way to Banff, she makes Dad stop at a place called Yo-Ho Kicking Horse Campground. That night we grill hot dogs and eat supper at a real picnic table that is in a big, round wooden pavilion. A family who speaks French eats their supper at the other end of the pavilion. The mom waves to us and says, "Bonjour." Mom waves back and says, "Hello." D'Nelle pipes up with her own "Bonjour." The night is magical, and I'd like to stay at Yo-Ho Kicking Horse forever.

We've now traveled for five weeks, and we're about to return to the United States. Dad has a golf game in Montana this afternoon. The long line of cars in front of us moves slowly. Each U.S. bound car stops, and the driver says something to the U. S. border guard, and then the car gets to move on. I feel sad about leaving Canada. Other than sharing a tent with eight people and dog, it's been lots of fun. The mountains around Shiprock are small hills compared to the Canadian Rockies.

Last week I touched a real glacier. I saw a moose and several bears. One night, Granddad waited until we were all asleep and then stood beside the tent and growled like a bear. Lady nearly broke her neck trying to jump through the tied door of the tent, trying to get the bear. Granddad laughed and laughed, and Dad cursed and cursed. I didn't think it was very funny.

When our car finally reaches the front of the line, the U. S. border guard slowly circles our car twice before leaning down to Dad's window. He says in a very official voice, "Sir, how long have you been out of the States?"

Dad turns his head so he won't blow cigarette smoke into the guard's face. "About five weeks."

The guard waits for Dad to look at him. "Was your visit to Canada business or pleasure?"

Dad flashes one of his famous ear-to-ear smiles and says, "Pure pleasure—played golf every chance I got."

The guard stares into the back of the car. "Sir, would you please pull your car into the parking spot on the left and have everyone get out of the car."

Dad isn't interested in chatting with the border guard. "Why?"

The border guard rests his hand on the top of his holster, stands tall, and repeats his request. "Sir, please pull your car into the parking spot on the left and have everyone get out of the car. Now."

I knew it—the lady who sold the bag of cherries to Mom this morning told her we couldn't take them into the U.S. Now we're all going to get arrested because Mom is trying to sneak them in anyway.

We pile out of the car and stand in an awkward line. Granddad takes off his cowboy hat and holds it in front of him. He looks madder than a skunk but holds his tongue. Lady doesn't know how to stand in a line, but Deanne's hand on top of Lady's head signals her to at least be still.

The border guard walks past each of us and stops in front of Mom, who is holding Mike, and Marilynn, who is holding Danny. He calls down to the front of the line to Dad. "Sir, who are these two young boys traveling with you?"

Granddad loses control of his tongue. "Oh, for Christ's sake."

The border guard's eyes shift to Granddad and then back to Dad.

Dad doesn't understand the question. "What do you mean, who are they? They're my sons."

The border guard walks back to Dad. "Well, sir, they look an awful lot like Eskimos. You know it's illegal to steal an Eskimo. Do you have some proof that these boys are your sons?"

Dad looks down the long line at Mom. She says in a frightened voice, "Yes, we do. It will take me a minute to find the adoption papers." Mom climbs into the back of the car and starts moving things around so that she can get to the right suitcase. One of the first things she tosses aside is the bag of cherries.

The border guard resumes questioning Dad. "Sir, do you know that it is illegal to bring that bag of cherries into the U.S.? Would you like to eat them or give them to us?"

Dad grabs the bag of cherries from the car and starts handing them out to us by the handful. He looks at the border guard and smiles.

Mom searches and searches, and we sit on the grass near the guardhouse and eat red cherries until our stomachs ache. Dad's not going to pay for something and then give it to a bunch of border guards to eat!

Lady's mouth is red from eating cherries. My fingers turn bright red. Deanne's shorts have cherry stains from where she touched them with her fingers.

Dad is mad at Mom for taking so long to find the adoption papers. When we successfully gain the okay to enter the United States, Dad drives like a bat out of hell so that he won't miss his tee time at the country club. Within an hour the sounds of stomach grumblings fill the back of the car.

Deanne is the first to complain. "Dad! Dad! Stop the car! Hurry, Dad, stop! I've got to go. Let me out. Hurry!"

D'Nelle suddenly has to go. "Me, too! Let me out. Get out of the way!"

Dad pulls to the side of the road, and Deanne and D'Nelle bolt from the back door and run for the bushes. Mom runs with Mike and Danny following her. Marilynn and Joellen and I look for another direction to run. Granddad sits in the front seat and laughs his head off. Dad paces beside the car and repeatedly checks his wristwatch; there's still a chance he might make his tee time.

Joe in golf shoes with bucket of golf balls—Canada, 1962

12

Leaving Shiprock

Canada is a distant memory by the time I get home. Bonnie's parents did a nice job of taking care of our house. The schoolteachers compound is still empty—school won't start for a few weeks. No one is at the boarding school, either. There is a new gas station along the highway, and construction has started on the new Methodist church for Bonnie's dad. With the addition of the new police station and courthouse last year, Shiprock is beginning to look a lot like Uvalde, a real town.

Before we leave Shiprock, Mom and Dad decide to take us on a picnic to see the Rock with Wings. I know that the Navajo story of Rock Monster is just a story, but I've believed it all these years, and I can't wait to see where Monster Slayer killed the *Tse na'hale*. My pending departure from Shiprock feels like I'm abandoning the reservation. The thought of moving to a different school frightens me. The thought of having Marilynn and Granddad take care of me while Mom goes to college frightens me.

The thought of Mom going to school frightens me—maybe she'll like school better than she likes us. She hasn't been in school since she was fifteen—she graduated from high school early because she was so smart that she skipped two grades. I can't really blame Mom for wanting to spend the day with grown-ups rather than with Mike and Danny and Granddad.

Tufts of brown and yellow desert grass break through the sandy desert floor. The unrestrained, barren limbs of the mesquite bushes seem frozen in place, like painful silent screams. Deep arroyos, with secret passageways that lead to the home of Tse na'hale, stretch for miles from the base of the lava rock. The still air smells of dust and sheep droppings. Our car bounces in and out of the potholes in the narrow dirt road that leads to the base of the rock.

The pockets of my shorts bulge with my collection of precious arrowheads. Dad says I can only take two with me when we leave. I'm going to bury the rest at the base of the Rock with Wings and return one day to claim them. I've learned that in addition to my lucky arrowheads, I'll have good luck if I do not to kill a spider or harm a lizard. I have been very careful all week to not kill a spider or step on a lizard; I want to have lots of good luck when I talk to Monster Slayer so he will watch over my arrowheads.

Swirling red dust settles around the car. Mom warns all of us to stay within her sight and to watch the sky for any signs of a sudden afternoon thunderstorm. If that happens, the small arroyos that surround the base of the mountain will fill with water. She bribes Mike and Danny into staying in the back of the car by plying them with peanut butter and jelly sandwiches.

Danny occupies himself inside the car by crawling around on his knees, trying to catch a giant black horsefly that keeps bumping into the car's window. Mike sits by the sack of peanut butter sandwiches and starts in on them.

Near the car, Deanne shadows D'Nelle. D'Nelle is sick of Deanne. She turns and yells at her, "Go away! Get lost! Scram!"

Deanne's right hand is in a plaster cast. Last week she picked up a big rock and tried to throw it at D'Nelle, but instead, she tripped and fell and broke a bone in her hand. Mom drove her to Cortez, and Deanne cried the whole way. Mom blames D'Nelle for the accident, so now Deanne knows she can follow D'Nelle around and pester her, and Mom won't stop her.

D'Nelle hurries to catch up with Joellen. Marilynn stops dead in her tracks and turns to scream at D'Nelle. "Am-scray. You are not coming with us."

D'Nelle looks around for me, but I hide behind a big rock. I can see her, but she can't see me. Deanne stands with one foot behind her, ready to go in whichever direction D'Nelle goes. D'Nelle sits down on the hot ground and reads her latest *Nancy Drew* mystery. Deanne is at a loss for what to do. "Come on, get up," she wheedles. "Let's play. Come on, D'Nelle. Mom, D'Nelle won't play with me."

I watch Marilynn and Joellen hurry behind a house-sized boulder and quickly whip out the March issue of *Teen* magazine that Marilynn has managed to never return to the bookmobile. I know they are going to read the lead article, "Why teens can't stop giggling."

Mom busies herself confining Mike and Danny to the car. She quietly practices saying out loud the new words that she's learning from the little dictionary she purchased at the grocery store in Farmington. She raises her eyebrows and smiles at Mike and Danny, as if she's telling them a story, and says, "Flatulence—that's what Lady has a lot of. Flatulence."

I'm confident that she will be the smartest mother of seven in college.

Dad grabs his bucket of balls and heads in the opposite direction from us. A little practice with his new sand wedge is just what he needs.

Before anyone sees me, I hurry away from the sounds of my family in search of Monster Slayer. I sit on my butt and slide down into a deep arroyo. Unconcerned about how I might get back out, I don't even pay attention to where I am. Thorns from dried mesquite tear at my legs and hands. Rocks and dirt follow me into the ditch, causing centipedes to wiggle to new holes, dragonflies to collide with my red shirt, and ants to invade the sides of my sneakers. A hawk screeches overhead, alerting Monster Slayer of my presence. Lizards scurry on the ground in front of me, leading the way.

The arroyo becomes deeper and deeper and more and more narrow. At times, I have to turn sideways to continue. I whisper to Monster Slayer as I walk, "I am here. Please guard my arrowheads for me."

I find the perfect hiding spot under a small lava rock. With my arrowheads safely buried, I stand and smile at the towering cliff above me. I try to memorize every rock and bush so that I will recognize my hideout when I return one day. I sit on my small lava rock and cry. I know that I'm getting older and going into the fifth grade, and I know I should act like a good Navajo and accept what's happening, but I just want to scream and yell and refuse to leave. I can't imagine living anywhere but Shiprock. I don't want to behave like a traditional Navajo and accept what happens and find the good in it.

I want to stay in Shiprock and enter the Miss Navajo contest. I want to join the junior high school band and play a trumpet. I want to go to high school with Bonnie and ride the bus to Kirkland with all of my friends. I'm not ready to leave. I close my eyes and send Grandma another letter:

Dear Grandma,

I'm so afraid. I don't know what's going to happen. Nothing will be the same. I don't want Mom to be a schoolteacher. I want her to stay home with me. Will you know where we are when we leave?

PART V

Navajo Taboo: Do not lie about yourself or bad things will come true.

○ ○

John F. Kennedy is assassinated. There are fifteen thousand U.S. military advisers in South Viet Nam.

Navajo Annie Dodge Wauneka is awarded the Presidential Medal of Freedom.

13

The White Man's World

When our red station wagon and Granddad's white Buick stop in front of our new rental house in Maricopa, Granddad is furious. He slams the Buick's car door so hard that Danny begins to cry. Granddad leans down and yells through my opened car window, "Goddamn it, Jo Eva! I'm not poor white trash. I've been poor most of my life, but I've always lived on the right side of the tracks!"

I try to figure out why Granddad is so mad. Is it because this is the only house on this side of the railroad tracks? The town, such as it is, and all of the other houses are on the other side of the railroad tracks. Granddad is also angry because on our drive through Maricopa, he notices that there are more Mexicans living in Maricopa than live in Uvalde.

I think that having a house on the wrong side of the tracks makes our house special; there's no one around us. The house doesn't look as nice as our Shiprock duplex, but Dad said that this is the house that the last coach lived in, and it was good enough for him so we're moving in. After he says this, Marilynn quietly mumbles, "Well, he didn't stay here, did he?"

It's a good thing Dad didn't hear her. It is odd that there is absolutely nothing around us except weeds. On our way into Maricopa I saw green fields and lots of small wooden houses. I wonder how far my new school is; I've always walked to school. Maybe this year I'll ride a bus.

Once we unload the car and the U-Haul trailer, it's easy to see that the house isn't much to talk about. In my old house I had to share a room with just Marilynn and Joellen. Now all us girls will share a room, Granddad and the boys will continue to share a room, and Mom and Dad will share. Dad says that I have to walk one mile to school. I have no idea how far one mile is.

Mike and Danny, Maricopa, 1962

Each morning, Dad takes the car and leaves early. Marilynn walks my sisters and me to school, and then she walks a little bit farther to her new high school. When we all get home from school each day, Mom takes Granddad's Buick and drives to Phoenix for her school. She stays late into the night and also goes to school on the weekends.

On our daily walk to school we pass fields of green plants, but no one can tell me what is growing in the fields. All of the land around Maricopa is planted and irrigated and plowed every year; we've moved to farming country. Behind our rental house there are no houses or planted fields or anything; it's just weeds and dirt as far as I can see. I see a coyote there shortly after we move in. There is not a fence around our house, so Dad doesn't let Lady outside unless one of us goes with her and makes her stay close to the house so the coyote won't eat her.

I wish I had Lady with me now to protect me from the coyote. It's late, but I'm so mad at Dad that I ran away to the backyard. Mom's not home from Phoenix yet, and everyone else has gone to bed. I sit on the ground behind our house with my back leaning against the wall to my bedroom. Earlier, I heard D'Nelle's and Marilynn's voices through the window. D'Nelle was convince Marilynn to go outside to look for me, but Marilynn only said, "Good riddance!" Joellen calmed D'Nelle and told her not to worry.

Fear creeps into my bones—I see the orange eyes of the coyote watching me. The weeds in the fields surrounding our house are so high that it's hard to see him, but I know he's there. I know it's not the same coyote that lives in Shiprock, but I know that if I write a letter and tell Bonnie that a coyote lives behind my house, she will write back and tell me to be sure I don't cross its path because that's bad luck. I don't know where the coyote goes at night, so maybe I've already crossed its path.

I'm still too mad at Dad to go inside. Last week, Mom promised me that I could march with the high school band at this week's football game. I play drums with the high school band because there isn't a band for the junior high school, and the high school band needed a drummer. I've spent weeks practicing with the band, and now that they are traveling to a school for an away football game, Dad refuses to let me ride on the bus with a bunch of kids from the high school. I don't know what the big deal is; Marilynn will be on the bus.

The window above my head slides open, and Joellen whispers, "It's okay. You can come in now. Everyone is asleep."

The next afternoon I stand my ground in front of Dad and say, "Mom said I could play with the band. You have to let me march with the band."

Dad is just as stubborn as I am. "I'm not the one stopping you from marching. Mr. Blake, your band teacher, said you were too little to carry the snare drum; that you can't keep up with the rest of the band. You can still play when the band is at the high school, but you're not going to march with the band."

I can't believe that Mr. Blake said those things about me. He told me that I scored one hundred percent on the rhythm test—that's why he picked me to play in the band. I try another tactic with Dad. "But Mom can give me a ride to the game and keep an eye on me, and I can just be with the band."

Dad shakes his head no. "Your Mom's still in Phoenix. You know she can't get here in time. Now just drop it—you're not going."

I can't just drop it. "But what's the use of playing drums in the high school band if I don't get to march with them?"

Joellen puts her arm around my shoulders and pulls me away from Dad. "Drop it, Danalee. We don't get to go to the football game, either. Be happy you're playing in the band."

My back is to Dad, so I don't realize that he can hear me say to Joellen, "It's not fair. How come Marilynn gets to go to the game? She's just gonna sneak off and kiss Ramon."

Marilynn shoves me in the back and whispers, "Shut up."

Dad grabs Marilynn by the arm and spins her around to face him. "Marilynn, I told you to stop seeing that boy. Are you sneaking around behind my back?"

Granddad loves to pick on Marilynn. "She's gone from injuns to wetbacks. Can't you even raise your girls to like white boys? She—"

"Shut the fuck up!" Dad yells at Granddad, even as he continues to stare at Marilynn. He turns to me. "Danalee, is Marilynn still seeing Ramon?"

I stare at the floor, afraid to look at Dad or Marilynn. "I don't know. I don't think so."

Dad levels his gaze at Joellen. "Joellen? Is Marilynn seeing Ramon?"

Joellen is braver than I am, and she looks Dad in the eye. "I don't know, Dad. I haven't seen her with him since you told her to stop."

Dad looks at the three of us and considers whether or not we're lying. Joellen is pretty convincing. "Okay, Marilynn," he says. "You can go to the game, but you're riding on the team bus with me, and if you are out of my sight for more than one minute, you're not going to another game this year. Go get ready."

I try not to look at Marilynn when she passes me. I know I'm in big trouble. I know she and Ramon plan to meet at the game, and I know she's still seeing him. Why can't she just pick a regular old boyfriend so Dad will be happy?

Dad's team wins football games just as easily as Dad wins golf tournaments. The only thing that slows down his winning streak is the weather. A week after the football game that caused the big argument between Dad and me, Maricopa is under a flood watch. Just like I had to do in Shiprock, I now stand in a long line in the school's cafeteria and wait to get a tetanus shot. For two days, water surrounds the school and the highway—it's so much water that Mom stays in a motel near Arizona State University. She stays up all night to study because she couldn't get home.

Every Saturday, Mom takes all of us with her to ASU. She has two classes that meet in the morning and while she's in class, we hang out at ASU. On the first Saturday of each month, the school shows a Walt Disney film in a room of the library. Today we will see *Sleeping Beauty*. All of my new friends saw this movie years ago, but I've never been to a movie, and I can't wait. Marilynn and Joellen sit in the back of the room, by the door, so they can take Mike or Danny out of the room if one of them gets noisy or scared. D'Nelle and Deanne and I rush to the front of the room to get as close as we can to the screen; the room is very crowded.

After the movie we visit the library so we can stay inside the air-conditioned building as long as possible. The books in the library smell wonderful. The rows and rows of books in the Arizona State library feel like home. The Saturdays that Mom takes us to school with her are the best.

Joellen stands behind me and whispers in my ear. "Come on, Danalee, let's go. Everyone is outside waiting for us."

I hate to leave the library. "Just a minute."

Joellen whispers in my ear. "You can't check out any of these books. You're not in college. What are you looking at? Come on. They're waiting."

I search the pages of a book called *Look Homeward, Angel*. On the back cover of the book, it says that the book is about a young boy who leaves home to find a better life. I think I'll ask Mom to check it out for me. I whisper to Joellen, "You guys go ahead and start walking to the Dairy Queen without me. I'll catch up with you."

I quickly examine the other books on the library shelf in front of me; finally, I leave. I walk fast to catch up with my brothers and sisters and think about how amazing it is that Mom is going to college. This is almost worth leaving Shiprock for. So far, the number one thing that is worth leaving Shiprock for is that Mom and Dad don't fight as much. I think they even like each other again. Early in the morning I can hear them making noise in their bedroom. This didn't happen as often when we lived in Shiprock. Dad gives Mom a kiss in the morning before he leaves, and Mom squeezes Dad's behind when she thinks none of us are looking.

When I reach the Dairy Queen, Marilynn is getting ready to order Dilly Bars. Each Saturday, Mom gives Marilynn thirty-five cents for seven Dilly Bars and enough money for seven nineteen-cent hamburgers. We always eat the Dilly Bars first and come back later for the hamburgers. When I approach the group, Marilynn hands me a nickel and says, "Everyone hold out your hand. Today, you can each order your own Dilly Bar."

She hands my sisters and brothers their own nickels. We form one long line of seven at the outside window of the Dairy Queen. Marilynn stands beside each of us as we order our very own Dilly Bar. Joellen and I order chocolate. D'Nelle and Deanne order butterscotch. Mike orders cherry—red is his favorite color. The lady takes his nickel but doesn't give him his Dilly Bar. My sisters and I start eating before the Dilly Bars melt.

Marilynn pushes Mike to one side and leans across the counter. "Miss? Excuse me, miss. He needs his Dilly Bar."

The black-haired lady doesn't look at Marilynn when she says. "Yeah, yeah. I'll get it." She takes the Dilly Bar from the freezer and lays it on the hot metal countertop, just out of Marilynn's reach. After a few minutes Marilynn leans across the counter and grabs the melting Dilly Bar, takes off the paper covering, and hands it to Mike.

Mike hands it back to Marilynn. "It's melting!" he cries.

Deanne offers Mike her butterscotch Dilly Bar. Deanne is in second grade now and is learning to tell the difference between when people are teasing Mike and Danny for fun and when someone is just being mean.

Mike considers the Dilly Bar and then says, "But it's not red. I want a red one."

Danny tugs on Marilynn's shorts and complains, "I didn't get a Dilly Bar. I want a Dilly Bar."

Marilynn sighs and leans across the counter again. "Miss, we need another cherry Dilly Bar."

The Dilly Bar lady again doesn't look at Marilynn. She says in a hurried, angry voice, "Sorry, we're all out."

Danny cries and stomps his little foot on the hard sidewalk. "I want a Dilly Bar. I want a Dilly Bar."

I hear Marilynn say under her breath, "Bitch." To the rest of us she says, "Come on, everyone, give me your Dilly Bars."

Marilynn collects the half-eaten Dilly Bars and smashes them onto the metal counter. The woman inside says, "Well! Just what I'd expect from a bunch of nigger lovers."

Marilynn takes Mike's and Danny's hands and walks away. "Let's go to the grocery store today and buy candy bars instead of old Dilly Bars. You can choose whatever kind of candy bar you want."

If I wasn't a chicken, I'd yell at the Dilly Bar lady, "We don't want your stupid Dilly Bars, you ugly white bitch!" That's what I'd say if I weren't a chicken. I'm surprised Marilynn didn't say it.

We don't tell Mom and Dad about the Dilly Bar lady; we don't tell them lots of things about how people treat Mike and Danny when we go to the nearby park or take a walk around the block. Dad is always busy working with his football or basketball team. Mom hardly sees any of us anymore. She studies during the day when we are at school and is gone every night for classes. She got special permission to take double the number of classes, so she has to work twice as hard as the other students. Driving to and from Phoenix takes lots of time, and so when school is over for the year, Dad finds a job teaching sixth grade in a little town called Apache Junction, a town right by Phoenix. Mom will now be only ten minutes from campus.

Granddad thinks any house will be better than the house on the wrong side of the tracks, but as I stand in front of our new rental, I'm not so sure. Paint peels from the wooden siding and the window screens have giant holes in them. Dad says it's a two-bedroom house because none of the landlords he talked to with bigger houses wanted to rent a house to someone with seven kids and a dog. He had to tell our landlord that it was just him and Mom renting the house, so if the landlord shows up we are supposed to hide or tell him that we live next door.

In this eight-hundred-square-foot house, one bedroom is for Granddad and the boys, and one is for us girls. Mom and Dad will sleep in the living room. It does have the tallest tree I have ever seen, right in the middle of our front yard. This house also is walking distance from the swimming pool at the Mesa City Park. Every day until school starts, Dad plays golf, Mom goes to school, Granddad stays home, and we kids walk to the swimming pool.

Marilynn holds Mike's and Danny's hands while we walk, but once we arrive at the swimming pool, Joellen is in charge of Mike and I'm in charge of Danny. Marilynn spreads her towel over a lounge chair and sunbathes in her new black swimming suit.

Mike, Danny, and Deanne wear inflatable rings around their middles; the rest of us can swim. The first day we arrive at the pool, I can hardly believe the city lets us swim for free. The cool water smells funny, and it isn't as cold as the Frio River at Mama Austin's house, but it feels great to splash around in the water nonetheless.

A pudgy lady wearing a flowered swimming suit interrupts Marilynn's sun-bathing. The lady shades her eyes from the sun and says to Marilynn in a polite voice, "Honey, someone said you are in charge of those two little nigger boys in the pool. Can you have them get out now so we can let our children swim?"

I can tell by the look on Marilynn's face that she is sick of people calling Mike and Danny "niggers"; doesn't anybody know what an Indian looks like? I'm sick of it too. I'm twelve, and I can tell the difference between a Negro and a Navajo, and anyway, who cares if a Negro or a Navajo swims in the swimming pool? Danny and I walk through the water to where Joellen and Mike are standing. Joellen puts Mike on her back and swims into the deep end of the pool. I bounce Danny up and down in the water and keep my eyes on Marilynn. Marilynn never looks up at the lady; she just flips the pages of her magazine and ignores the woman standing before her.

The lady moves to the side of Marilynn's lounge chair and tries to get Marilynn's attention. "Hon, I'd like you to get those boys out of the water so my boys can get in."

Deanne stands on the step in the shallow end of the pool and yells, "Niggers! Come out, come out, wherever you are!"

I don't think Deanne remembers the Negros from the Globetrotter game in Window Rock. D'Nelle takes one look at Marilynn and dives to the bottom of the swimming pool and tries to sit on the bottom.

Marilynn lowers her magazine and gives Deanne her "I'll kill you if you say one more word" stare. She quietly tells Deanne, "Shut up and start swimming." Deanne dog paddles out to where Danny and I stand in the pool, and she splashes us with water. With Deanne hanging on to my right arm and Danny hanging on to my left, I walk into the deep end of the pool and strain to keep my nose above water. D'Nelle surfaces for a breath of air, surveys the situation, and then returns to the bottom of the pool. Joellen and Mike swim toward me, and I can tell from the look on Joellen's face that the lady standing beside Marilynn better watch out. Last year, Joellen punched a fifth grader in the nose for calling me "toothpick legs."

A mom with a little boy wrapped her neck swims up to Joellen and says, "Your little brother is going to be a strong swimmer one day. How old is he?"

Joellen, braced for a snide remark, lets her muscles relax. She smiles at the lady and says, "He's almost five. He can swim in the shallow end but not out here in the deep. How old is your little boy?"

Before the lady can answer, Deanne pushes away from my side and yells, "Look at me! I can swim!" She dog paddles back to the steps in the shallow end of the pool and jumps up and down on the top step. She calls out in a loud voice, "Rickety-rackety-ree! I see something you don't see! And it's blue and green, and D'Nelle is wearing it!"

Mike and Danny giggle. The woman and her son giggle. Deanne jumps up and down on the step and slaps the surface of the water with her hands. She smiles at Mike and Danny and says, "Rickety-rackety-ree! You can't see me." She holds her breath and sits on the bottom step.

Marilynn mumbles to herself, "Good."

The pudgy lady in the flowered swimming suit no longer bothers Marilynn; I don't see her anywhere. I guess she and her little boys left. The cool water of the swimming pool becomes our second home for the rest of the summer and every weekend during the school year. Just because Mom is closer to campus doesn't mean she stays home more often. Granddad complains that she is never around. Dad and Mom don't make noise in the mornings anymore. Mom stays up late into the night and sits at the tiny kitchen table, writing papers and studying for tests.

One year later, at the end of the summer term, Mom graduates with honors; all of the studying has been worth it. She makes all A's except for one B. I'm so proud of her. She doubled up on all of her classes and received her bachelor's degree in two years, twice as fast as all the other students. Dad doesn't want to stay around to watch her walk to the podium in her long gown; he wants to leave the minute her last class is over. Mom wants to walk to the podium and receive her diploma. I'm on Mom's side. The new teaching jobs they have in Nevada are on an Indian reservation outside of a town called Reno. I don't understand the big rush to get there. If Mom and Dad were going to get jobs on an Indian reservation, why didn't we just go back to Shiprock?

14

Reno, Nevada, 1965

Our rental house in Reno has a fenced yard for Lady and three bedrooms, so Mom and Dad no longer sleep in the living room. The reservation school is about a thirty-minute drive, so they leave early in the morning. Mike starts first grade this year, so Danny is left alone with Granddad. On our way to school, Joellen and I walk through a pasture that has a bull in it. We're pretty good about sneaking across the pasture without his seeing us. D'Nelle, Deanne, and Mike only have to walk about three blocks to their school. Marilynn rides to her new high school with the girl who lives across the street from our rental house.

Mom is very unhappy to be out of college. I think she would have been happy to stay in college and take classes forever. Teaching kindergarten is harder than she thought it would be; she's never had a job before. Sometimes I find her sitting at the kitchen table late at night, eating raw liver. The doctor says she's anemic and raw liver is the best way to get iron. Blood drips from the corners of her mouth when she chews on the liver. She pats my hand and tells me to go back to bed; there is nothing I can do to help her.

Mom has a secret friend that we aren't suppose to know about, but Granddad, Marilynn, Joellen, and I know. I don't think Dad knows about him, but Dad doesn't pay much attention to anything but golf. Her friend lives close by, and Mom can just walk over there when she's sick of listening to Marilynn and Granddad argue over what radio station to listen to, or Granddad's telling her she can't do anything right. I guess this friend knows how to help her.

One evening I sit on the front step of the porch and wait for Mom to come home from seeing her special friend. When she arrives, she sits down next to me and holds my hand. Her voice is soft. "Honey, you need to stop worrying about me. Sometimes things just get too crazy around here. I just need to visit with someone who is far away from all of this. I hope you can understand. Don't worry; I'm not having an affair. Remember when Dad thought I was having an affair when we lived in Del Rio, and he stormed off and took the job in Shiprock?

I don't want anything like that to happen again, so please, just help me keep my secret."

We sit on the step, and she holds my hand. I'm jealous that Dad gets to run off and play golf when he wants to get away from here, and now Mom gets to run off and visit a friend when she wants to get away. When do I get to run off?

A few days later I don't get to run off, but I do get to go with Dad and Marilynn and Joellen to the mall to buy some new school clothes. Mom's visiting her friend, and D'Nelle is babysitting Deanne and the boys while Granddad listens to his favorite radio station. Dad drives us to the mall and then waits outside the stores while we shop. We take a long time in the panties and bra store because the store people have a hard time finding a bra that will fit Joellen. We take so long that when we emerge from the store, Dad is ready to leave; he's had his fill of shopping.

When we reach the parking lot, Dad marches off ahead of us. Suddenly, he sits down on a wooden bench on the edge of the parking lot and grabs his chest. Two seconds later, he lies on the dirty asphalt and gasps for breath. Marilynn drops her shopping bags and rushes to his side. Joellen is frozen to her spot and screams, "What's wrong? Marilynn, what's wrong? What's wrong with him?"

Joellen's panic-stricken voice doesn't shut up. I run to Marilynn's side and stare down at Dad. Sweat pours from the top of his head. He's ghostly white. He can't breathe, and he's trying to tear off the front of his shirt. He whispers to Marilynn, "I'm … I'm …" But then he collapses.

A lady with a pink hat shoves some coins in my hand and tells me to run to the mall, find a phone, and call an ambulance. When I return, Marilynn and Joellen stand by Dad's head while a man in a blue shirt kneels beside Dad and unbuttons the buttons at the top of Dad's shirt. He keeps telling Dad, "Lie still. Take short, slow breaths."

An ambulance arrives, and two men load Dad onto a stretcher and put him in the back of the ambulance. While they load him in the red ambulance, one of the ambulance men asks, "Is your dad a veteran? Was he in the military?"

Marilynn mumbles, "He's a Marine."

Marilynn starts to climb into the back of the ambulance with Dad but the same man says, "Sorry, girls, you can't ride with us. Call your mom and tell her we've taken him to the Veterans Hospital. From the looks of him, she'd better get there as soon as she can."

The ambulance zips away, lights flashing and horn blaring. The man in the blue shirt walks back to the shopping mall. The lady with the pink hat stares at us. We stand huddled together, holding our shopping bags and wondering what to do. In the absence of a tissue, Joellen uses her shirt sleeve to wipe the tears and snot from her face. The lady touches Marilynn's arm and says, "You girls want a ride to the hospital? Come on, I'll drop you off there, and you can call your mom from there."

The waiting room at the Veterans Hospital has white plastic chairs. Marilynn calls Granddad and leaves a message for Mom. I know Marilynn knows where Mom is, but she won't call there. If Dad dies while Mom is visiting another man, Marilynn will hate her forever.

My sisters and I are the only ones sitting in the plastic chairs. The waiting area smells like antiseptic, flowers, and dust. A couple of old ladies, who wear pink-striped pinafores, repeatedly walk from the gift shop to the elevators. Back and forth, back and forth, a pink-striped lady delivers flowers to someone in the hospital.

We pool our money to see if we can buy Dad some flowers; we can't. Anyway, he doesn't like flowers. He likes chocolate-covered cherries. Each year for his birthday, he gets a box of chocolate-covered cherries. He can put three in his mouth at the same time and still talk.

The elevator makes a "ping" sound every two or three minutes. The lady who sits behind the information desk won't tell us where Dad is or what has happened to him. She says she'll only talk to Mom.

I wonder what will happen to us if Dad dies. Mom's teaching certificate hasn't arrived in the mail, so she can only teach on the reservation for now. Granddad is useless; he hasn't worked since Grandma died. Maybe Mom will take us back to Shiprock and live in the duplex. She could teach school there. Maybe Marilynn, Joellen, and I will have to get jobs in Reno. I can make fifty cents an hour babysitting. If Dad dies, I wonder if we can still move into the house that Dad and Mom just bought. It's being built and is supposed to be finished and ready for us to move into next month.

I don't think our house would be much different if Dad were dead, except Mom would be happier, and I wouldn't have to listen to Mom and Dad yelling at each other. I don't really want Dad to be dead, but I really would like it if they would stop yelling at each other. I've tried plugging my ears with my fingers, stacking pillows over my head, and humming to myself, but nothing really works.

When Mom rushes into the lobby of the hospital, her special friend is with her. Granddad knew where to find her. She is as white as Dad was. The lady behind the information desk tells Mom where to go and calls after her as she rushes away, "Those girls have to stay in the lobby. You're the only one allowed in emergency."

We listen to the elevator ping as the doors close on Mom. Her friend looks at the three of us and says, "Tell your mom I'll call her later and see how Joe's doing."

My sisters and I sit on the plastic chairs and wait. We are silent for hours. I guess if Dad was dead, Mom would have come right back. The elevator isn't pinging as often, and there's a new lady sitting behind the information desk when Mom finally walks through the doors of the elevator.

Mom looks like someone has punched her in the stomach. Marilynn, Joellen, and I still don't say anything, but we watch her slide into one of the plastic chairs. Tears pool in the bottom of her eyes. When she leans over to put her head into her hands, tears drop onto the dirty linoleum floor. After a while, she looks at us and smiles. "Well, girls, your dad's had a heart attack. It's a bad one—they think he'll be in the hospital for about two months, and then he'll have to take it easy for a while. He's supposed to stop smoking."

"Fat chance of that happening," Marilynn mutters.

Mom tries to smile at her. "I think you're right, but that's what he's supposed to do." She stares at the dirty floor. "The Veterans Hospital won't let anyone under the age of sixteen go upstairs to his room."

Marilynn sits up straight and announces, "Well, then, I can go." She sees the look on Joellen's and my face and says, "Don't worry; I'll find a way to sneak you upstairs."

Mom stands up and gets ready to leave. "Who has the car keys?"

Marilynn also stands and stares at Mom. "Dad."

Mom is perplexed. "What?"

Joellen finally speaks. "A lady gave us a ride to the hospital. The car is still parked at the mall."

Mom starts walking toward the elevator. "Wait here, and I'll go up and get the keys. Marilynn, call Skeet and tell him to let D'Nelle watch the kids. Tell him to drive down here and give us a ride to the mall so we can get the car."

Halfway to the elevator, she turns and shakes her head at us. "You let a stranger give you a ride to the hospital? You guys know better than to get in the car with a stranger."

It's been two months since that horrible day. Dad is coming home from the hospital tomorrow. We moved into our new house while Dad was in the hospital. All of the houses on our block are new, and each house on the block either looks like our tri-level or the two-story house that is next to ours. Each house is painted a different color, but they still all look alike.

Dad says that when he feels better, he's going to divide the basement in our new tri-level house into three bedrooms. The new house has three bedrooms upstairs—one for Marilynn, one for Mom and Dad, and one for Granddad. Marilynn fought hard to get her own bedroom. She begged Mom, saying, "Mom, I'm the oldest. I'm in high school. I do all of the cooking and cleaning. I deserve my own room."

At the moment, the rest us all sleep in one big room in the basement, but when Dad remodels the basement, D'Nelle and Deanne will share a room, Mike and Danny will share a room, and Joellen and I get to share a room. This is the best house we've ever lived in.

The only bad thing about having a bedroom in the basement is the smell of the laundry. Joellen and I sleep next to the space in the basement with the washer and dryer, and until Dad builds us a wall, we have to look at the pile of dirty laundry and smell it.

I think Mom likes the house, but she is still sad all of the time. She can no longer just walk to her friend's house and have some quiet time. She spends a lot of time at the hospital with Dad. Sometimes, we go along and Marilynn sneaks us into Dad's room by walking us up a back staircase. We have to then walk on the floor where all of the crazy people stay, without letting the nurses see us, and then go up one more flight of stairs to Dad's room. Mom likes it when we are there with her.

Granddad is very happy to have his own room, and he stays in it a lot. Marilynn stays in her room and plays records. Mom stays in her room and cries. Mom's room is directly above Joellen's and my area in the basement, and when Mom isn't working or visiting Dad, Joellen and I can hear her crying through the heating vent. We lie in bed and listen to her but don't know what to do to make her feel better.

When Dad comes home from the hospital, he continues smoking and counts the days until he can return to the golf course. Within a month, he returns to work and returns to the golf course. One weekend, he devotes all of his time to remodeling the basement, and Joellen and I finally have our own bedroom.

Now that Mom has a job, we're all supposed to share the chores, but when it's Marilynn's week to do the laundry, it never gets done. On Monday mornings before school starts, I have to dig through the pile of clothes and find my dirty PE clothes and stuff them in my backpack for another week of classes. Our new house is far away from Marilynn's high school, so she now rides a bus to school.

Joellen and I walk to junior high school, and D'Nelle, Deanne, Mike, and Danny all walk to their elementary school. Joellen stays after school every day and practices with the band; I like walking home by myself.

One day after school, I see Danny running ahead of D'Nelle, Deanne, and Mike. When I catch up with them, they tell me that Danny is mad because a girl in his classroom won't be his Valentine because he's an Indian. None of us are as upset as Danny; I guess we've all just accepted, at some level, that some people are weird about Indians. Even Mike has figured this out. My brothers are the only Navajo in their school; I think they are the only Navajo in Reno. The kids at Danny and Mike's school think it's funny to call them names or to push Danny around on the playground. Mike is already so big, no one pushes him around.

Not everyone in Reno is like that, but I can just tell when an adult doesn't like them by the way he or she looks at them, or when they put their arms around their children and steer them away from Mike and Danny, as if being near them would cause some illness. Fortunately, there is only one family on our street that refuses to let their kids play with us; no one else seems to mind.

When we reach home, Danny stands in front of Mom. "Please, Mom! Please call Susan's mom, and tell her I'm white. I have a white mom and a white dad. Please, Mom, call her."

Mom has heard this plea before from Danny. "I'll do no such thing. It's just a silly Valentine's card. Forget about it."

Danny follows her around the room. "Please, please, please. Mom. Tell her I'm not a nigger or an Eskimo; I'm white. She knows you. She knows you're white. Please, Mom, I want Susan to be my Valentine. Please, Mom."

D'Nelle, Deanne, Mike, and I quietly sneak off to the basement. We are all chickens. On my way downstairs, I watch Danny crumble to the living room floor and cry, "Please, Mom, please!"

I'm angry that Mom doesn't help Danny. There must be something we can do that will make him feel better. Mom says to ignore people who act like Susan. Dad says, "You're white. You're living with a white family." I wish I could think of something to say or do that would make Danny feel better. In the end, it turns out not to matter, because Danny doesn't go to school on Valentine's Day—but then, none of us does.

In January, Granddad's coughing grew worse; he was keeping Mom, Dad, and Marilynn awake at night. Mom and Dad fight about him all of the time. Three months ago, when the doctors told Granddad that he had lung cancer, he made Mom promise to let him die in his own bed. He hasn't gotten out of his bed since then. He's just waiting to die and be with Grandma. Each evening I try a get him to eat some soup, but he just wants to die, and I guess I want him to die, too. He's waited a long time to see Grandma again.

I am the only person Granddad tolerates. I try to feed him, change his pillow-case, and turn the radio on and off each day. I clean up the mess he makes when he coughs up blood. I think Mom and my sisters would do this if they could, but Granddad hates everyone else. I suppose I could stop doing it, and then Dad would take Granddad to the hospital, but Granddad wants to die at home, so I'm trying to help him do that.

One night, a few days before Valentine's Day, Granddad and I listen to Jim Reeves sing on the radio. Mom and Dad come into his bedroom and ask me to leave. I try to look into Mom's eyes, but she won't look at me. I stand beside the bed and hold Granddad's hand and won't leave. Dad pushes me aside, and he and Mom put some jeans and a wrinkled shirt on Granddad and try to make him stand up. He can't.

Dad says, "Shit." He leans across the bed and lifts Granddad under his arms, and Mom lifts Granddad's bare feet. Dad backs through the bedroom door and down the hallway, talking to Granddad the whole time. "I'm sorry, Skeet, but it's time you were in the hospital. You're too sick for us to take care of you."

My mind can't function fast enough to comprehend what is happening. They are really taking him to the hospital, even after they promised him they'd let him die in his own bed.

Granddad whispers through the coughs that tear through his boney body, "Danalee, help me. Help me."

That's when I stop being a chicken. I shadow Mom's step and try to stop her. I yell, "Stop! Wait! You promised! Mom, stop! You can't do this. Please. Please, wait."

My brothers and sisters stand at the bottom of the stairs. No one else yells for them stop. I know Marilynn can't wait to get rid of Granddad. Mom and Dad carry Granddad outside to the driveway and shove Granddad into the backseat of the car. They won't let me climb in beside him. The last I see of Granddad, his tall, skinny body is folded like an accordion, smashed into the backseat of our car. He dies in the hospital the next day, alone and betrayed.

The only person in the house who tries to talk to me in the days that follow Granddad's death is Joellen. She talks to me, and I hear her—but I don't hear her. My mind is numb. I don't understand why Mom betrayed her dad. Dying at home was all he wanted to do. It didn't seem so hard to let him just die. Mom tries to talk to me before we leave for Uvalde to bury Granddad in his family's plot, but I don't have anything to say to her.

Before we leave for Uvalde, Dad buys a new pickup truck and puts a camper cover over the bed of the truck. Then he connects the camper with the cab of the truck by installing a leather boot on the back window. Mom buys a wooden yardstick that she shoves through the window and waves around in the air when we get too noisy. She can't really hit any of us because all we have to do is lie flat on the floor of the truck, but she likes the power of waving it around.

Dad puts an old couch in the camper part of the truck and builds wooden covers to go over the tire wells, so someone can sit there and look out the side windows. It's a nice arrangement, and I wish I could be more excited about it, but I'm not excited about anything.

I wonder if Granddad ever woke up. I wonder if he knew he was in a hospital. I wonder if he hated Mom for not letting him die in his own bed. Maybe it doesn't matter. Maybe he's already with Grandma, and it doesn't matter how he got there. I hope he's with Grandma.

It will take three days of solid driving to get to Uvalde. Granddad's body travels on an airplane. It's only the first day of our drive, and Marilynn and D'Nelle spend their time arguing over who gets to sit on the wheel well. Marilynn thinks she gets to do whatever she wants, just because she's the oldest. They resort to shoving each other on and off of the seat. Mom pokes her wooden yardstick through the window's boot and starts waving it around. Everyone dives for the floor.

When the stick retreats, Marilynn beats D'Nelle to the wheel-well seat. I sit in the one seat in the back of the truck where Mom's stick cannot reach—in the corner directly behind her. She'd have to break her arm to get it to bend in my direction. I look around the truck and wonder what it must be like to live in a family that has only two children. Sometimes it feels like a small army follows me around. I can't get rid of any of my brothers or sisters, but now I'll live in a house without Granddad. I wonder what it will be like.

Granddad's funeral takes place on the day after we arrive. We stay in the backyard of Big Mama's house, but now we are all older and our bodies so much bigger than the last time we stayed in the yard. It feels like we are smashed together in a big box at bedtime.

I know Granddad and Grandma lived in Uvalde when I was a child, but Granddad never talked about that time. I wonder who will come to his funeral—and why.

The funeral home's interior is dark and musty. An old lady dressed in black plays the organ, while people stream in and fill the small room to capacity. I have no idea who all of these people are. I recognize old Dr. Eads; he's really old. He's the doctor who delivered Mom, Marilynn, D'Nelle, and me. It's exciting so see so many people come to Granddad's funeral, but I wonder why I'm just now learning about Granddad's friends.

I sit in the back of the funeral home, in the little room reserved for family. The walls are papered with purple velvet cloth. There are five church-like pews for family members to use as they wait for their turn to kiss the corpse. The pews have worn brown material on the backs, and they smell like tobacco. My sisters and cousins take turns going up to Granddad's coffin and kissing him good-bye. I don't need to kiss him good-bye; he's already gone.

Marilynn nudges me in the back. "Go on. It's your turn. Hurry up."

I stand in front of the coffin and stare at the powder-covered face of the man inside. He smells like the frogs I dissect in science class. His false teeth crammed into his mouth make him look like someone I don't know. I am humiliated for him. I lean close to his cheek but do not kiss him. I whisper in Granddad's ear:

"Dear Grandma,

Here's Granddad. He's missed you for a really long time. Please take care of him."

After the funeral we drive out to the cemetery where Vice President John Nance Garner is buried. Granddad and the vice president's son were once close friends. Granddad's family plot is just below the vice president's family plot. The plot is calm and shady. Granddad's father and stepmother have big granite head-stones that occupy the center of the plot. Granddad is going to be buried in the top corner of the plot, near a juniper bush. I stare at the empty gravesite next to his and wonder when Mom will have Grandma's body moved from El Paso to Uvalde, like she promised she would.

The cool February air of the cemetery smells better than the old pews of the funeral home. Most of the people leave the gravesite by the late afternoon. Dad and Uncle Bob stand far away from Granddad's family plot and talk about sports. Mom and Aunt Betty wander off, but I can still hear them.

Mom's voice is angry. "Goddamn it, Betty Jean, give them back to me."

Betty Jean's voice is just as angry. "No. Papa wanted me to have them."

I reach the site of the big argument. Mom grabs for the things in Aunt Betty's hand. She screams in her sister's face, "Liar! You were standing right next to me when he told us Mama's wedding rings were for Danalee. Now give them to me!"

Betty Jean struggles to keep the rings in her clenched fist. "I don't remember any such thing. You've been smoking peyote with your injun friends."

Mom stands back and stares at Aunt Betty. "Betty Jean, I'll take them from you; you know I can. Papa's not here to save you this time."

Mom grabs Aunt Betty's arm and begins to twist it. Aunt Betty and Mom have attracted a crowd. When Aunt Betty sees Uncle Bobby, she switches to her helpless, poor-me voice and cries, "Ow! Ow! Let go of my arm! Bobby! Bobby! Jo Eva's gone crazy. Help me."

Uncle Bobby rushes to Aunt Betty's side. He wraps one arm around Mom's slender waist and lifts her off the ground and away from Aunt Betty.

Mom wiggles and squirms and hisses, "Betty Jean, you bitch! I'll never speak to you again."

When Aunt Betty, Uncle Bob, and my cousins leave the cemetery, we load up the car and leave for Reno. Mom is still so angry, none of us want to risk talking to her. Riding in the back of the truck on the way home feels like none of us will ever speak to each other again. My siblings and I sit on the old couch, the wheel well seats, and the floor of the truck, thinking our private thoughts. It's hard to imagine our house without Granddad.

I know that when I walk through the door of our house, the odor of Granddad's cigarettes will linger in the air. His clothes will still hang in his bedroom closet. His precious mandolin will rest on the top shelf of the closet. But Granddad will not be there. I'm glad he won't be there. I guess if I went to church, someone might tell me that I'd go to hell for being glad that Granddad's dead, but Granddad has wanted to be dead ever since Grandma died. I think it's okay that he finally got his wish.

I sit in the corner of the pickup truck and stare out the window and watch the desert zoom by. This part of Texas looks a lot like the land around Shiprock. Big, puffy white clouds hang in the sky. I stare at them and look for Granddad and Grandma in the shape of the clouds, just like I did in my secret hideout in Shiprock. I look around at my brothers and sisters to see if anyone else is interested in the shape of the clouds.

I watch Mike and Danny roll the center of a slice of bread into a tiny ball. I realize that Danny is only five, and Mike is six—they probably won't remember Granddad at all, so I shouldn't worry about all of the mean things he said to them. The clouds in the sky outside my window suddenly look like Granddad and Grandma. I smile to myself. I'm surprised that there are still times that I wish I was back in Shiprock, with the freedom to run to my secret hideout and lie on the trunk of a giant cottonwood tree and watch clouds. But I am not in my old hideout or even in Shiprock. Next year, when I start high school, I won't ride the bus with Bonnie to Kirkland. I'll ride to school with Joellen and her boyfriend. My high school in Reno will have almost a thousand kids in it, so I will get to see how the kids in the Shiprock boarding school felt.

I look forward to high school. Marilynn likes her new high school, and all of her boyfriends are white—of course, all of the boys in the school are white. Dad doesn't complain about any of the boyfriends she brings home. He doesn't meet too many of them because he's always at work or the golf course. Last fall, he worked really hard and turned our backyard into a putting green and two sand traps. Marilynn, Joellen, and I take turns pushing the heavy mower across the putting green each day so that it is in perfect putting condition for Dad, whenever he wants to go outside and putt for a while.

Granddad told Dad that he was a complete fool for ripping up the backyard, but he's not around now to complain anymore. He can't call Mike and Danny dirty injuns or yell for Deanne to get Lady away from him. I no longer have to listen to Marilynn and Granddad fight nonstop over which television channel to watch or which radio station we will listen to.

Joellen and I get to move into his old room. We're going to paint it bright blue. It will be exciting, living upstairs with Marilynn, Mom, and Dad. Without Granddad around, Dad might even stay home more and talk to us. Now, Dad doesn't have to pretend that he didn't hear Granddad call Mike or Danny a dirty injun. Maybe he will help me figure out how to deal with people who call Mike and Danny names. I know that my sisters and I can't fight with every single person who calls them nigger, Jap, or Eskimo. People are just going to have to learn to recognize a Navajo when they meet one.

The clouds outside my window shift again and now resemble Shiprock. I search the dark regions of the cloud for something that looks like Monster Slayer. Deanne sits beside me on the old couch and looks at me with her ocean blue eyes. "Danalee, is Granddad in heaven?" she asks. I can feel everyone's eyes on me, waiting to see if I'm going to burst into tears and scream at her to go away or do something else. Strangely, I am not sad; I am relieved to know that Granddad is with Grandma and that I won't have to take care of him anymore.

I smile at her and say, "Yep! I'm pretty sure that Granddad and Grandma are up in heaven right now, looking down on you." I tickle her tummy. "They're probably smiling and wondering if I can make you laugh." I continue to tickle her. Mike comes to sit next to a giggling Deanne and waits for me to tickle him, too. Danny is close behind. D'Nelle puts down her book and helps me tickle the three of them. I stop tickling them and tell them, "Granddad is in heaven right now, laughing and laughing. He's happy to be with Grandma. They're both going to watch over us and make sure we are happy."

I watch the clouds reform into something else. Like the white puffy clouds, everything changes. I will try to be a good Navajo and accept my life without Granddad and Grandma. I will find something good to think about. Maybe I can help Danny convince Susan to collect Easter eggs with him since he missed the Valentine's Day party; that is something good to think about.

Epilogue

The Navajo believe all things are connected and that it is the responsibility of each person to help maintain a sense of harmony and order in ones daily life. This sense of harmony is often referred to as *hozhoni*. Following the death of my grandfather, my parents, sisters, brothers, and I each followed our own paths in search of *hozhoni*. I think the death of my grandfather was the first step for each of us to move out from under the cloud of his unhappy life and look for happier times.

When I think of my childhood home, I think of Shiprock. I smell the dust, see the boarding school playground, and hear the horseflies buzz near my ears. I see Brother Frank wave to me from the porch of the Catholic mission. I was happy there. I like the desert. I love the Navajo. I can't imagine life without Mike and Danny's being part of it, but I have a much better understanding of the difficulties of mixed-race adoptions.

I'm pretty sure that my parents had absolutely no idea what the creation of a mixed family would bring. By adopting Mike and Danny, I believe that my mother behaved in a way that I hope most people would have done—she saw a child who needed love and care, and she didn't give one thought to the color of his skin. Unfortunately, we live in a society where people do respond to skin color. Adopting a child with a different ethnic background than ones own requires thinking about how to best balance that child's culture with the culture of the adoptive family.

Mike never had the opportunity to know his half brother, Kevin. Although Danny eventually met some of Mary's other children—his biological siblings—others died before he had a chance to know them. As young children, Mike and Danny knew nothing of their Navajo heritage because my parents never shared that with them. I don't know if understanding something of their culture would have eased the pain of the prejudiced teasing they endured, but I do know that telling them that they were "white," just because they lived with a white family, didn't work. In fact, I believe that telling a child to pretend he is white implies that being white is better than being any other race. In a mixed-race adoption it's the parents responsibility to help their child learn to appreciate his uniqueness and ensure that he feels loved for who he is, regardless of the color of his skin.

When my family returned to the white man's world in the summer of 1962, my sisters and brothers and I were ill prepared for life off of the reservation. Marilynn struggled to fit in with her new teenage friends because Marilynn's life experiences were different than most of her peers. From the day my grandmother died, Marilynn's childhood vanished, and she assumed the duties of an adult. She ruled the house with an iron fist, helping to raise all of her siblings, while being hell-bent on maintaining some small bit of freedom for herself. She mothered her sisters and sometimes even her own mother, and when Mom and Dad divorced in the early 1970s, Marilynn provided the kind and loving support that Mike and Danny desperately needed.

Marilynn and Joellen followed in our mother's footsteps and married as soon as they graduated from high school. I jumped ship by moving away and going to college. As soon as D'Nelle and Deanne graduated from high school, they, too, had a similar compulsion to leave town as fast as they could. At that time in our lives, we were all escapists, even Mom.

Shortly after Deanne graduated from high school, Mom began an affair—for real this time. She left home, divorced Dad, and later remarried. The marriage lasted a couple of years. She had a series of relationships following her second divorce, but none made her happy.

Her experiences—being a teenager when she married Dad and the unexpected and sudden loss of Doris—weighed heavily on her behavior as a parent. The burden of caring for her father left her angry and often struggling with her own depression. As she's aged, she's developed strong ties with Marilynn; they now have the time to enjoy the relationship they missed during Marilynn's childhood.

Mom kept her promise to her sister, Betty, and didn't speak to her again for thirty-eight years. By the time she did, Betty's struggle with senile dementia meant that she didn't recognize her sister.

When Mom and Dad divorced in the early-1970's, my fragile teenage brothers bore the brunt of Dad's anger, shame, and despair over his wife's abandonment. She left her teenage sons with a father who barely knew them. During their childhood years, he left the house early enough each morning to play nine holes of golf before work and allowed time after work for nine to eighteen more.

Mom reasoned that because Mike and Danny were boys—and boys with athletic skills—Dad would make some effort to interact with them. I was married and living in another town at this point, but I knew this was just a rationalization on her part—although I wanted it to be true. After the divorce, Mike and Danny had the good fortune to have Marilynn and Joellen continue their roles as surrogate mothers. As the only sisters who lived in Reno at the time of my parent's divorce, Marilynn and Joellen attended their basketball games, cheered for them at track meets, did their laundry, and made suppers for them.

Marilynn continued the role she began at age twelve—taking care of her siblings; she tried to explain to Mike and Danny why Mom had to leave. Mom faced a difficult choice: stay in her marriage and continue to be unhappy, or leave and take a chance on a new marriage—and hope that Dad would become a more active parent to Mike and Danny. She thought she had years to help her sons understand her reasons for leaving. She did have time to reconcile with Danny; Mike didn't live long enough for her to do the same with him.

Like many children of divorce, Mike became very protective of Dad. He felt Dad's pain and tried to reconcile Mom's betrayal. Excelling in sports offered a path to my father's heart. An outstanding athlete, Mike spent his junior high and high school years setting state records for distance running.

The summer before his senior year of high school, Mike interned with a group of archeologists from Harvard University who were working at a site in the hills outside of Reno. Shortly after school started for his senior year, he received a letter from Harvard, inviting him to apply and offering him financial assistance. Unfortunately, Harvard's offer held little value for Dad. In his worldview, boys joined the military after high school; they did not go to college.

Mike traveled to Portland, Oregon, where I lived with my husband, and we spent a long weekend discussing his options. I knew how Mike felt. It hadn't been so long ago that I had breathlessly waited for Dad to say something encouraging to me. I understood how it felt to be trapped by what he'd like to do and what he felt obligated to do. At the age of seventeen, Mike still very much wanted to gain Dad's love and approval. He still believed he could do something that would make Dad say, "Great job, son. I love you."

After graduation, Mike joined the army, and after four years in the army, he returned to Reno. He got a full-time job and began working his way through college. He and Marilynn and Marilynn's husband met each Friday after work for a beer. One Friday in December 1975, Mike did not show up. Marilynn's search revealed that he was not at his apartment, his job, Dad's house, or Joellen's house. He'd vanished!

Initially, the police took a familiar attitude toward Mike's disappearance: "Just another drunken Indian"; "Probably ran home to the rez"; "Anything missing from your house? Go on home; he'll turn up when he runs out of money."

My sisters and I had lived our childhoods dealing with such perceptions of Mike and Danny, just because they were Indian. The reaction from Reno's police didn't surprise us, but it did repulse us. Our brother was missing! We didn't need taunting remarks; we needed to find Mike. When Dad got involved in the search process, the police stepped up their activity, but no one could find any trace of Mike. Nearly four months later, when the Truckee River began to thaw, Mike's waterlogged, battered body surfaced.

Jammed between two logs, his defrosting body left the city's medical examiner baffled. It was hard to determine if Mike had been beaten before he went into the water, of if the motion of the two logs against his body had caused the extensive damage.

His undisturbed wallet led the police to conclude that robbery was not the motive. Mike was not drunk when he hit the cold waters of the Truckee River and had not accidentally fallen in. Had someone pushed him? Although the phrase "hate crime" had not surfaced in 1975, we wondered if some guys had beat up the "injun" and tossed him in the river, just for fun. Mike died at the age of twenty-three. It felt as if he'd lived a millisecond. The suddenness with which he was yanked from my life made it difficult to believe he was gone.

My siblings and I sat in the front pew of a small funeral home in Reno, staring straight ahead. Danny, now in the army, seemed more alone than any of us—his brother and the only Navajo in his world had just died. The funeral service dragged on for an eternity. A minister, who'd never met Mike, spoke words meant to be comforting; they weren't—Doris, Skeet, and Mike were together in heaven, and somehow I was supposed to keep living on earth.

In death, Mike regained some small part of his Navajo heritage. In Navajo tradition, when a Navajo nears death, his body is placed outside the hogan to die. When he dies, the body is wrapped and often placed in a high place before being cremated; his ashes are left to rejoin their place with Mother Earth. Mike's battered body was cremated; his ashes were spread among the hills in which he'd worked the summer of his junior year in high school.

Danny's life started falling apart long before Mike's death. He never mastered Mike's skill of believing he was white, just because Dad told him he was. As a child, he wanted to be white but lacked the emotional skills to ignore the taunts, name-calling, and social snubs. Every "nigger," "Eskimo," and "dirty injun" pierced his heart. At the age of eight, he sat in the bathtub and rubbed his skin raw in an attempt to make it whiter.

Like Mike, he excelled in sports. He broke all of Mike's state records for distance running, and by the age of fourteen, he ran close to a four-minute mile.

This remarkable feat led him to compete in the tryouts for the Junior Olympics in the fourteen- to eighteen-year-old category for the mile. I traveled to Sacramento to watch him run.

The California sun spread out across the track, and by the late afternoon, runners competed in ninety-degree temperatures. Danny's race fell late in the afternoon. Dad hammered him all morning on the best strategy for the race. Danny half listened; the field of competition included runners Danny delighted in watching.

He ran a good race. As a fourteen-year-old competing against the size and strength of eighteen-year-olds, Danny didn't have much of a chance, but he was thrilled to be there. Dad missed the point of being thrilled to be there. He had a fourteen-year-old son who ran close to a four-minute mile, and he failed to acknowledge that other older and more experienced runners also ran close to a four-minute mile.

Like Mike had before him, Danny still believed that he could do something of which Dad would approve. If running close to a four-minute mile didn't generate approval, maybe joining the army would do so. Danny quit high school, left home, and joined the army.

After the army he returned to Shiprock, to his Navajo family. He met his mother and brothers and sisters and learned of his older sister who had not survived life on the reservation. He struggled to learn the language. A newly found uncle performed a Blessing Way to help cleanse the white man's ways from Danny's spirit.

In the mid- to late 1970s, not unlike today, life on the reservation for a young adult Navajo usually involved alcohol and drunken fights. Sadly, Danny became like many of the other young adult Navajos who lived on the reservation; he became an alcoholic. He was involved in knife fights and permanently lost several teeth before he found the strength to leave the reservation and change his life.

He stopped drinking and stopped fighting. He's made a life for himself in a town off of the reservation but remains close enough to see his Navajo family. He's finally discovered a way to reconcile his white and Navajo worlds. He has a white family who loves him and whom he loves, and he has a Navajo family who loves him and whom he loves. After years of struggle and the loss of his brother Mike, Danny has discovered his own *hozhoni*.

My father retired as an elementary school principal and moved to a small town in Arizona; he bought a house on the edge of a golf course fairway. For the remainder of his life, he played golf every day, and he eventually met a woman who loved golf as much as he did. I realized that they'd gotten married because one year, my Christmas card from Dad was signed "Dad and Mrs. Joe Mitchell."

I met his new wife a few times. She lovingly cared for him through five years of the heart-related illness he suffered before his death. Once dementia claimed his mind, and he could no longer play peacekeeper between his wife and Danny, her complete intolerance of her Navajo stepson halted Danny's weekly visits. My father died at the age of seventy-seven. All of his children except D'Nelle who was ill, traveled to Arizona for his funeral. We sat through talks from his neighbors about his kindness and generosity, and I wondered who this man was, who my father had become. I certainly would not have described him as kind or generous.

When I was a child, he spent much of his time wanting to be anywhere except with us. I'm glad he spent the last years of his life on a golf course, the place where he found the most happiness. I don't think he found that kind of happiness with Mom or with any of his seven children. By the time I was eighteen years old, I had stopped waiting for Dad to accept me.

After high school I returned to Mesa, Arizona, and attended Arizona State University, the first college I'd seen and home to the library I'd loved as a child. During my father's conference trip to Phoenix, we planned to meet for dinner. Excited about the possibility of actually spending some time together, I cooked dinner for him and even stretched my food budget to purchase his favorite chocolate-covered cherries. Dinner was at 6:00 PM; his golf buddies dropped him off at my place at 11:00 PM, drunk. I listened to him complain about my mom, my sisters, my brothers, his job, and his lack of time to play golf. At 1:00 AM, I drove him to his hotel and left him with a box of chocolate-covered cherries. On the drive home I was, strangely, not angry or sad; I was just relieved. It was as though my adult life came into focus, and I realized that I no longer needed Dad to say "great job" or "I love you." What he thought of me no longer seemed important. As if I'd experienced my own version of a Blessing Way, I cleansed myself of needing Dad's love or approval. I incorporated the Navajo philosophy of acceptance, loved my father for who he was—and moved on. I no longer worried about a coyote crossing my path, I found my own *hozhoni*, a sense of balance and harmony in my life.

978-0-595-40543-5
0-595-40543-6

www.ingramcontent.com/pod-product-compliance
Lightning Source LLC
Chambersburg PA
CBHW020415290526
45785CB00002B/579